Servants, Slaves, and Savages

Servants, Slaves, and Savages

Reflections of Law in American Literature

Veronica C. Hendrick

CAROLINA ACADEMIC PRESS

Durham, North Carolina

Library of Congress Cataloging-in-Publication Data

Hendrick, Veronica C.
Servants, slaves, and savages : reflections of law in American literature /
Veronica C. Hendrick.
p. cm.
Includes bibliographical references and index.
ISBN 978-1-59460-442-3 (alk. paper)
1. American literature--African American authors--History and criticism.
2. Law and literature--United States. 3. Slavery in literature. 4. Law in literature. 5. Indentured servants in literature I. Title.

PS153.N5H466 2012
810.9'896073--dc23   2011052718

CAROLINA ACADEMIC PRESS
700 Kent Street
Durham, North Carolina 27701
Telephone (919) 489-7486
Fax (919) 493-5668
www.cap-press.com

This book is dedicated to Thomas Connors, Ph.D.,
Jacobus Schmidt, Ph.D., and Fr. Lawrence Wrenn, JSD in thanks
for their continued support and encouragement.

Contents

Acknowledgments

Support for this project has come in various forms, all of which have been immensely helpful. Therefore, I would like to offer my thanks to the following institutions and individuals for their support and encouragement.

I would like to thank the City University of New York for awarding me two separate grants that enabled me to take two courses off from teaching to devote to my research. I would also like to thank John Jay College of Criminal Justice (CUNY) for supporting me with an in-house research grant which supplied me with books and materials.

Through support from the National Endowment for the Humanities I was able to devote 6 weeks to research as a participant in the summer seminar conducted by Joseph Miller, entitled *African Dimensions of the History and Cultures of the Americas*, held at the University of Virginia and The Virginia Foundation for the Humanities. Through support of the Institute for Constitutional History, under the superb leadership of Maeva Marcus, I have been able to attend research seminars that have informed this and other works. Similarly, I would like to thank Allison Pease who, through a grant from The National Endowment for the Humanities, brought a series of speakers to the English Department at John Jay College of Criminal Justice (CUNY) and included me in these faculty research seminars focusing upon the field of Literature and Law.

Additionally, I would like to thank the following two institutions and their organizers for supporting my research through grants and seminars that allowed me to present my work in earlier drafts. The first opportunity came through a two-year grant that supported my attendance in an ongoing working group housed at The Gilder Lehrman Center for the Study of Slavery, Resistance, and Abolition at Yale University, conducted by David Blight, Paul Finkleman, and Jenny Wahl. The second opportunity was presented by the New York Law School's Legal History Colloquium, conducted by Daniel Hulsebosch and William Nelson. I was able to present a completed manuscript for comment and would like to extend a special thanks to Rebecca Bratspies, R.B. Bernstein, Bernard Freamon, Harold Forsythe, and William Nelson for spotting problems and sharing their insights.

Servants, Slaves, and Savages

Reflections of Law in American Literature

Introduction

As one reads through various forms of American literature, perhaps all bodies of literature for that matter, the ever present force of law makes itself known in subtle yet significant ways. Recent works of fiction situated in the war torn world of Iraq and the detainment camps at Guantanamo Bay easily connect to their military and legal contexts; however, as one moves back through American history and the novels which describe culturally significant events, the inherent connections to the legal structure informing these narratives are often lost. Much of this slippage is problematic only to the historian, more specifically the legal historian, who appreciates the nuanced development of judicial and legal policy and who cringes when the details of such shifts and changes are muddied or misrepresented in literary renderings. It is not, however, just the specialist who profits from well crafted, historically factual narratives that inform while they entertain, enlighten while they enrich.

It might even be argued that it is the general reader who is best served by narratives that employ social, political, or legal analysis. Whether intended or not, these forms of narrative help stave off the diminishing connection to American legal history. If law and history can be unearthed from the narratives and used to contextualize a work, then literary interpretations using these frames as analytical tools can offer an enriched and enriching rendering of novels, autobiographies, poems, or other narrative structures.

Various forms of American literature comment upon the legal status of workers and residents, but none are as provocative as the literature discussing slavery and enforced servitude. Whether the literature is an autobiographical account or a contemporary novel, narrative impressions of slave/servant laws are powerfully translated. Through the poetry of Sojourner Truth, the narrative of Frederick Douglass, or the fiction of Toni Morrison, images jump from the page to become active accusations against slave laws. Equally compelling are the historical underpinnings leading to the development of codes and laws which dictate the rights, or lack thereof, of servants, slaves, and Native American people in the colonial and early American periods.

In order to discuss the various intersections of forces that codify the status of individuals within the early American period, this work investigates three distinct yet interrelated areas of American law: the laws of slavery, the laws of servitude, and the laws governing Native American people who often straddle the divide. Although literature does not neatly divide itself according to these categories, a combination of autobiographical and fictional accounts has been selected for this purpose. These accounts reflect or comment upon particular laws that are useful for understanding the stratified system that developed as the nation evolved from a colonial possession into a fledgling, then established, nation. These selections tell stirring tales that are fleshed out in five separate chapters: 1) *Legislated Inhumanity: The Expanding Separation of European Indentured Servants, African Slaves, and Native Americans;* 2) *Reflections of Law in Slave Narratives/Slave Narratives Influencing the Law;* 3) *American Legacies: Slave Laws and Envisioned Lives;* 4) *The Laws of Indentured Servitude: Fact and Fiction in American Literature;* and 5) *Native American Enslavement and Other Legalized Brutality.*

The introductory chapter, *Legislated Inhumanity: The Expanding Separation of European Indentured Servants, African Slaves, and Native Americans,* provides the framework upon which the ensuing chapters elaborate. Although literary material is used to highlight and exemplify various issues, the intent of the first chapter is to outline the historical and legal issues which influence the status of these three groups. The chapter begins with the historical backdrop to the laws of servitude and reflects upon English Common Law and practices. The indentured servant system and the related processes of the apprentice and redemptioner systems trace their roots to the English law. Similarly, the English exportation of political prisoners, convicts, vagrants, and debtors through the indenture systems is outlined. Brief discussions of pirates and their enslavement of Europeans are included in this section. The chapter then focuses upon the employment conditions in colonial America and the arrival of the first Africans to Jamestown, Virginia in 1620.[1] Some of the historiography analyzing this period suggests that the initial status of these 20 African people may have been on a par with that of European indentured servants; however,

---

1. 1620 is recognized as the year when a group of 20 Africans landed upon Virginia shores. There was a much earlier presence of Africans in other colonial territories, such as the Spanish territories of Florida.

a series of laws were quickly enacted which made the distinction between the two groups increasingly rigid. Literary representations are used to animate some of the court cases and laws enacted which solidified this division. The chapter closes by focusing upon the experiences of Native American people and the laws which dictated their status within the nation. The intention is to outline the happenings in the nation and the development of various laws and programs that codified the status of the Native people. The often ignored enslavement of the Native American people as well as tribal participation in the slave trade are outlined and further elaborated upon in the book's final chapter. The earliest treaties are discussed as antecedents of the notorious actions of the Jackson Administration. Although literary references are peppered throughout the introduction, the majority of this section relies upon historical and legal events. The four chapters which follow this opening analysis are rich in their treatment of literature and its intersections with law as both a reflective agent and an agent of change.

The second chapter, *Reflections of Law in Slave Narratives/Slave Narratives Influencing the Law,* focuses upon slave narratives which comment directly upon the laws that dictate the status of Africans and their decedents within the colonial and early American periods. The two significant qualities of slavery, its inheritability and its permanency, are constant points of emphasis within this body of literature. These features, and how they come about, differ from other colonial arrangements and dominate the narratives of the period. The spread of slavery and its development as a race based system are equally significant. Many of the autobiographical accounts of life within the race based slave system pay particular attention to the status of mixed raced children. Frederick Douglass and Harriet Jacobs focus particularly upon the law which dictates that the slave status is inherited through the maternal line despite the free status of the paternal figure. Both Douglass and Jacobs are intimately influenced by such unions: Douglass believes his master fathered him along with his brother and sister, and Jacobs herself gives birth to two children fathered by her white/free lover. These writers quote the law directly and decry the situation of children whose master is also their father. The reflection of this and other laws discussed in slave narratives is an exciting topic for analysis; nonetheless, a second aspect of slave narratives merits equally enthusiastic investigation. This chapter delves into the influence literature has upon the development of law. Slave narratives were instrumental in the abolitionist movement. Both the written accounts and the writers themselves captivated the public imagination. The prime example of this is Frederick Douglass: his presence on the speaking circuit and his involvement in the *North Star* propelled him into the limelight and moved the abolitionist cause rapidly forward. And, although this chapter includes an analysis of Frederick Douglass in his role as political spokesperson, other writers helped sway the mood of the public.

One of the most recognized pieces of literature focusing upon the laws of slavery with the expressed intent to change the laws of the country is that of Harriet Beecher Stowe's *Uncle Tom's Cabin; or, Life Among the Lowly*. In this work, Stowe presents the characters of Senator and Mrs. Bird to make comment upon the recently passed Fugitive Slave Act of 1850. This well-established couple is living in the South, and Senator Bird has just returned from voting in support of the establishment of the Fugitive Slave Act. His horrified wife makes comments about the appalling nature of the slave catching industry as well as the cruelty this new law would engender. In quiet conversation with her husband, she doubts his ability to carry out the actual practice of the law despite his theoretical approval. In this section, Stowe's social commentary cannot be missed. Not only does she step out of the narrative on multiple occasions to directly address the readership and implore it to fight against slavery, but she also provides overly calculated instances in which her narrative fulfills her social agenda.

In this instance, Senator Bird's words have barely been uttered when he is confronted by the reality of the law he has supported. Upon his doorstep arrive the beautiful young slave, Eliza, and her son, Harry, who have clearly just fled from bondage. Just as Mrs. Bird had predicted, the Senator is unable to follow the dictates of the Fugitive Slave Act. He cannot relinquish Eliza to the slave catchers pursuing her. Instead, he undertakes great personal risk by conveying Eliza and Harry to a location where he knows she and her son will be conducted further north to safety and freedom.

In this work, Stowe takes great pains to explain the particular hardship faced by slave women. Stowe directs her comments to the free women of the North, and she begs their pardon when discussing the sexual vulnerability of women within slavery. It is no accident that Stowe has selected/created a beautiful mulatto woman as the subject of her discussion. By using Eliza as the light-skinned embodiment of the slave system, Stowe hopes to connect her readership to the experiences Eliza suffered. Stowe's dependency upon pigmentation and affiliation is an uncomfortable undercurrent employed to support her lofty agenda. Stowe is a woman of her time, and embedded in her work are found many examples of racist attitudes. Nonetheless, the overriding value of this particular work is its direct comment upon the injustices of law, the hypocrisy presented in Christian principles when they are applied to slaves, and the overriding horror created by the American dependency upon slavery. A final point of significance is that Stowe does not leave the Northerners out of her denunciation.

Stowe not only condemns the profiteering enjoyed by the northern industrial leaders, she also condemns the misguided attitudes of northern people. Stowe links the position of northern individuals to that of the southern slaveholders and deems both unpalatable. Furthermore, Stowe attempts to demonstrate that there is no such thing as a benevolent form of slavery. Even the most kind and compassionate masters described in her novel come under scrutiny for their complicity in the larger system. Stowe's work built upon the popularity enjoyed by the writers of slave narratives and became the most popular novel of its time. With a similar abolitionist agenda, the work of Stowe connects to the writings of Frederick Douglass and Harriet Jacobs.

As vital as slave narratives are to the discussion of literature and slave laws, fictional accounts of slavery hold equal footing in the modern context. Therefore, the third chapter, *American Legacies: Slave Laws and Envisioned Lives*, focuses specifically upon fictional accounts of slavery. The growing body of fiction set in the antebellum South connects to the long tradition of American writing; consequently, the laws and conditions of slavery presented in this fiction reflect the ramifications of slave law on American culture and society. One particular legal action that is vividly and consistently represented in fiction is the Fugitive Slave Act: runaway slaves, passage along the Underground Railroad, slave tracking and recapture have seized the popular imagination for well over one hundred and fifty years. Next to Stowe's *Uncle Tom's Cabin* stands Toni Morrison's Pulitzer Prize winning novel, *Beloved*. However, lesser-known works are woven into the fabric of this chapter to exemplify various slave laws.

Another aspect discussed in this chapter is the way in which modern writers have erroneously imagined the conditions of slavery and the legal situations of the age. By highlighting such discrepancies between fact and fiction, especially within contemporary novels, modern cultural perceptions of slave law can be corrected. An additional advantage in studying modern novels focusing upon slavery is their inclusion of outside groups. They often include figures other than African slaves in their representations. For example, it is common to have a minor character who is either a European indentured servant or an enslaved Native American. The treatment of such minor characters and the differences in status ascribed to them by contemporary writers reflects modern understanding of the legal realities. Interestingly, and quite problematically, many observations presented in such works become part of the discourse on slavery regardless of their accuracy.

The fourth chapter in this analysis of literature and law is an often overlooked topic: indentured servitude. The chapter *The Laws of Indentured Servitude: Fact and Fiction in American Literature* discusses autobiographical monographs and fictional accounts of life within the indentured system. The laws related to contracts and obligations of both the servant and master are outlined. Issues of 'head rights' and Freedom Dues are discussed, as are the personal limitations impressed upon indentured servants. The illegality of servant marriage is one such topic. Another is the problematic situation presented by unplanned pregnancy, which also had legal ramifications. A further consideration is the implication for free individuals who married slaves, which could result in their entering into an indentured servant-like contract for the lifetime of their spouse. Later, such unions would become wholly illegal. As mentioned earlier, many novels reflecting upon slavery include peripheral characters of indentured servants and enslaved Native Americans. But more significantly, almost all tales of indentured servitude include images of slaves.

An example of this is found in *The Infortunate: The Voyage and Adventures of William Moraley, an Indentured Servant*, a text first published in 1743. Within the looping tale of his descent from titled gentry to indentured servant, the narrator sets up the stark contrast between the condition of servants and slaves in the British colonies of North America. And, although Moraley himself proves to be quite an unreliable narrator, he nonetheless offers valuable perspectives on the various types of servants and slaves found in 18th century colonial America. In addition to Moraley, the letters and memoirs of indentured servants are used to discuss the legal conditions servants faced in the colonial and early American periods. This chapter also investigates other aspects of European servitude in the Americas as well as briefly touching upon literature reflecting white slavery and the particular plight of women captured in the Cromwellian "cleansing" of Ireland. However, the bulk of this chapter discusses the laws and conditions of indentured servants reflected in the literature of the period as well as modern interpretations.

The fifth and final chapter, *Native American Enslavement and Other Legalized Brutality,* outlines the legal status of the Native American people during the colonial period and various policies of relocation that led to the reservation system. Literary imaginations often ignore the enslavement of Native American populations and the active involvement of several tribes in the slave trade. Therefore this chapter explores equal parts of literature and history to develop ideas and connections. When the European settlers decided that Native Americans were problematic slaves, the settlers began a process of deportation and sale of Native American slaves to the West Indies, primarily Barbados. Although I have not found any narratives that focused strictly upon this condition, there are representations of minor characters in fictional accounts. This chapter presents the various early laws related to the rights of native people and focuses upon land rights, forced marches, religious coercion, and relocation. The works which offer themselves up to this analysis are both first person narratives as well as fictional representations.

In total, the intention of this book is to provide an analysis of selected material that links the plight of three groups who suffered because of their legal status. The definitions that describe an individual as a servant, a slave, or savage had massive repercussions on the conditions of individual lives. The codes and policies which differentiated these groups had legal significance which ultimately influenced the method of their incorporation into the US citizenry. Treatment meted out to individuals within the legal system was inherently tied to their position within the hierarchical social structures and supported by the laws, policies, and treaties which bound them in service. The power of these definitions is emphasized by literary and personal narratives which comment directly upon the laws that effected laborers' lives.

Some of the most provocative work focuses upon the situation of women within these legal frames. The sexual and reproductive qualities possessed by women are highlighted as uniquely burdensome aspects of bound labor for female laborers. Sexual abuse and forced reproduction are presented in works that focus upon the conditions faced by slave women as well as works that focus upon the plight of indentured female servants. The sexual vulnerability of women is less focused upon in the Native American fiction presented than it is in the other works discussed. This may be due, in part, to the fact that the majority of Native American voices discussed in this volume are focused on larger corrosive aspects of the colonial and American influence. Issues of tribal power and sovereignty become topics of Native American literature when these narratives comment upon US policy and law.

In total, *Servants, Slaves, and Savages: Reflections of Law in American Literature* is offered as an overview of the disparate conditions experienced by European indentured servants, African slaves, and Native Americans while emphasizing commonalities shared among these groups during the colonial and early American periods. Some of the most salient points developed in this work focus upon the power of law and the strength of hierarchical structures. Through these engines of social construction, individuals and groups were categorized and defined in terms of their legal status as well as their claims to humanity.

Individuals involved in bound labor, either as a servant or as a slave, found themselves vulnerable to machinations which limited and at times threatened their lives. The systems which created and supported the conditions of bound labor were embedded in legal codes, some of which became manifest in policies that relegated certain individuals to the lowest rungs of society. The ramifications of these conditions and the legacies of these laws echo throughout the literature presented. Modern writers harken back to these conditions and trace situations to their characters struggling with parallel structures of oppression in contemporary times. Ultimately, *Servants, Slaves, and Savages: Reflections of Law in American Literature* presents connections among three groups of people caught in the problematic hierarchy of colonial and early America and focuses upon the legacy of these structures.

Chapter One

Legislated Inhumanity: The Expanding Separation of European Indentured Servants, African Slaves, and Native Americans

Virginia 1662-ACT XII. *Negro womens children to serve according to the condition of the mother*[1]

> *Whereas some doubts have arrisen whether children got by any Englishman upon a negro woman should be slave or ffree, Be it therefore enacted and declared by this present grand assembly, that all children borne in this country shalbe held bond or free only according to the condition of the mother, And that if any christian shall committ ffornication with a negro man or woman, hee or shee soe offending shall pay double the ffines imposed by the former act.* [Original spelling retained]

Maryland 1664. *An Act Concerning Negroes & other Slaues*[2]

> *Bee itt Enacted by the Right Honble, the Lord proprietary by the audice and Consent of the upper and lower house of thise present Generall Assembly that all Negroes or other slaues already within the Prouince And all negroes and other slaues to bee hereafter imported into the Prouince shall serue Durante Vita'*

Virginia 1705—ACT XXII. *An act declaring the Negro, Mulatto, and Indian slaves within this dominion, to be real estate*[3]

---

1. ACT XII. Negro womens children to serve according to the condition of the mother. 2 Hening (VA) 170 (Dec. 1662).

2. An Act Concerning Negroes & other Slaues. Proceedings and Acts of the General Assembly (1664). Assembly Proceedings (MD) 533 (Sept. 1664).

3. ACT XXII. An act declaring the Negro, Mulatto, and Indian slaves within this dominion, to be real estate. 3 Hening (VA) 333 (Oct. 1705.

*Be it enacted, by the governor, council and burgesses of this present
general assembly, and it is hereby enacted by the authority of the
same; That from and after the passing of this act, all negro, mulatto,
and Indian slaves, in all courts of judicature, and other places, within
this dominion, shall be held, taken, and adjudged, to be real estate
(and not chattels;) and shall descend unto the heirs and widows of
persons departing this life, according to the manner and custom of
land of inheritance, held in fee simple.*

Although slavery was practiced throughout the European colonies in
the Americas during the 17th and 18th centuries, the slavery system in
colonial America developed in ways that uniquely influenced the national
culture. By tracing the appearance of a few colonial laws, and the issues that
led to their creation, an understanding of this period is developed. Historical
data, court cases or public records, further flesh out the early moments
of American interaction with African laborers. From this evidence, it becomes resoundingly clear that what had first resembled a servant system
that paralleled the indenture servant system and echoed some of the features of the apprentice system rapidly degenerated into an increasingly severe system of slavery. The three legal shifts noted in the Acts of 1662,
1664, and 1705 are vibrant examples of the augmentations to the definitions and status of slaves. The impact of these changes comes alive in the
literature of the 19th century.

In discussing the Virginia Act XII of 1662, in which the slave status became inherited through the mother, the writing of one particular ex-slave,
Harriet Jacobs, exemplifies the ramifications of such a shift in law. In her
work, *Harriet Jacobs: Incidents in the Life of a Slave Girl*, 1861, Jacobs vividly
details the subjection she sufferes as a sexual target. By delving into the
episodes of her sexual assault, as well as the assault on her motherhood,
the law which provided for such abuse can be opened to analysis. In a similar fashion, the work of Frederick Douglass can be used to discuss the impact of both the Virginia Act of 1662[4] and that of 1705,[5] in which slaves
were defined as property. *The Narrative of the Life of Frederick Douglass,
an American Slave*, 1845, impressed upon the reader the inhumanity of
colonial American and US slavery. Emphasizing his status as property,
Douglass took particular note of the constant relocation of his person to

---

4. 2 Hening (VA) 170 (Dec. 1662).
5. 3 Hening (VA) 333 (Oct. 1705).

suit the economic needs as well as the personal whims of his owners. Not unimportant was the fact that Douglass was a mulatto: this Spanish and Portuguese word for mule was derisively used to describe a child born of one white and one black parent. Although Douglass was unable to provide evidence of his paternal blood, he was told that his father was white and all indicators lead to his conclusion that his owner was also his father.[6] Douglass' work, in combination with Jacobs' tale, highlights the vulnerability of slave women and the precarious position of children born of unions with white fathers.

The final Act to be fleshed out through American literature is Maryland's edict of 1664 from the Proceedings and Acts of the General Assembly,[7] which stipulated that slaves would be slaves for life. Although this seems to be a redundancy, as the term slave implies that the status is immutable and lifelong, it was in fact a necessary clarification. The ever-devolving status of African workers in the colonies created many ambiguities, and legislators were pressed to codify their definitions. Not only were there several institutions of servitude operating at the time, but there were also inconsistencies between the various territories in colonial America. Through the Maryland Act, the stage was set for other colonies to make slavery an inalterable inherited status. The inescapable quality of slavery, the fact that one was unwittingly born into the status and bound to it without reprieve, was accented in narratives of slavery. Yet, the slave narratives did much more than rail against the injustice of such a birthright; they created a call to action. The works of Douglass and Jacobs were cited as inspiration for, and tools of, the abolitionist movement on a par with Harriet Beecher Stowe's *Uncle Tom's Cabin*, 1852. Even after the goals of abolition were met, the literature of slavery continued to be produced. The flood of slave narratives continued to influence the development of legislation for many years after the US Civil War. Modern writers still retell the plight of slaves, and their body of work may influence current debates, such as the call for reparations due to the descendants of slaves.

As a backdrop to this discussion, it is important to understand several of the underlying features and problems in the history of colonial American/US slave codes. The way in which they developed and how they differed from other colonial arrangements were subtle. One distinction was that the slave laws in Brazil and other South American colonies were based

---

6. Thomas Satterwhite Noble's striking painting 'The Price of Blood,' 1868, portrays a mulatto slave being sold by his father.

7. Assembly Proceedings (MD) 533 (Sept. 1664).

upon Roman Codes of slavery, whereas the US system of slavery developed out of English Common Law. Although slavery was no longer practiced in England,[8] there was a firmly ensconced system of servitude. Various stratifications existed in Britain, and the servant class was well structured. The apprentice system, vestiges of which still exist today, informed the early American design; however, it was the use of indentured servants and redemptioners[9] that created the bedrock of the colonial system. Its English root which, given the influence of the Enlightenment,[10] should have made the American system more flexible and humane, may have been responsible for its development into an extremely rigid system.

Since the colonies of non-British nations had established codes of slavery, there existed, if only distantly, precedents and rules of conduct. Arguably, these codes prevented certain abuses. Although much colonial American slave law was part of South American colonial slave codes, the permanent, inherited status as chattel differed and the overall system of South American slavery was more malleable. Therefore, the status of a Brazilian slave was more fluid than it was for those in the US. For the South Amer-

---

8. Essentially, slavery ended in England by the close of the Middle Ages. The Cartwright decision of 1569 during the reign of Elizabeth I held that 'England was too pure an air for slaves to breathe in,' a phrase repeated in Lord Mansfield's 1772 ruling to free James Somerset, a relocated American slave fighting extradition. The Somerset case (R. v. Knowles, ex parte Somerset) formally abolished slavery in England proper. (For a full discussion of the Somerset case, see Wiecek, William M. 'Somerset: Lord Mansfield and the Legitimacy of Slavery in the Anglo-American World.' 42(1974) *The University of Chicago Law Review* 86–146.); This case also led to the abolition of the Slave trade throughout the Empire in 1807, the same year the United States ratified its law to cease the importation of slaves, which was enacted in 1808. Slave holding, however, continued in the British colonies until much later in the 19th century: this practice was viable in the Caribbean until 1834 and in India until 1861 (Schama Simon *Rough Crossings: Britain, the Slaves and the American Revolution.* Ecco New York 2006).

9. The redemptioner system differed from indenture in that the travelers tended to pay a portion of their fare prior to expatriating and hoped to pay the balance upon arrival in the colonies. The money could be acquired upon arrival through trade, through the help of family members, or a prior business arrangement (Hendrick, Veronica. *Codifying Humanity: The Legal Line between Slave and Servant* (2006) 13 Texas Wesleyan Law Review Fort Worth).

10. The Enlightenment movement and its antecedents proclaimed the ideals of 'good sense, benevolence' and the belief in liberty, justice, and equality as the natural rights of man. For an interesting discussion of the enlightenment and slavery, see Diggins, John P. 'Slavery, Race, and Equality: Jefferson and the Pathos of the Enlightenment' (1976) 28.2 American *Quarterly* 206.

ican colonies that absorbed the roman laws, the process of manumission was a straightforward and commonplace occurrence. Because of the relative normalcy of a slave's promotion to free status, many of the people freed in South American colonies remembered their own or a parent's role as slave: equally important was that many South American slaves had realistic hopes for freedom. This fluidity, as well as other factors of slavery to be highlighted below, created a distinctly different institution of slavery in South America from that of the US. And, whatever similarities did exist throughout the Americas evaporated once colonial America began to define and legislate slavery.

The disorder found in the slave system of colonial North America had much to do with its ambivalence toward the concept of slavery. Because this system of slavery developed out of the British system of indentured servitude, the initial scenario was multifaceted. The problems began in the early 1600s, when the colonies were in desperate need of labor and actively recruited servants from Europe.[11] In order to entice workers, passage to the colonies, room and board, and either land or financial rewards were promised. These rewards became known as Freedom Dues. In exchange, the workers would contract out their labor for a specific period of time. As the need for labor became increasingly desperate, due to the rapid increase in the demand for colonial goods and the economic potential open to entrepreneurs, the amount of land promised, as well as other Freedom Dues, increased. As a further financial incentive, all employers who brought new workers to the colonies were granted land or other goods. These rewards were based upon the number of imported people, or "heads," that the employer pulled into the colony's work force and became known as head rights. Fifty acres of land, or sometimes one hundred acres in Maryland, were given to anyone who paid a laborer's passage to the colony.[12]

---

11. See Galenson, David W. *White Servitude in Colonial America: An Economic Analysis*. Cambridge University Press New York & Cambridge 1981.

12. Head rights were also allotted to free Africans: 'In 1664, Anthony and Mary Johnson appear in the Northampton court records, two of the 62 Africans listed among the 450 odd "tithables" on the tax lists. From 1664 to 1677, there were 13 free African householders living in Northampton, including Anthony and Mary. When Anthony and Mary reappeared in the historical record, they had four children and claimed 250 acres of land due them for five head-rights of either persons who were indentured servants on their estate or persons from whom they purchased their head-rights. One of the persons, Richard Johnson was probably their son.' See the National Park Service (NPS), U.S. Department of the Interior website for other court cases involving slaves: http://www.cr.nps.gov/ethnography/aah/aaheritage/Chesapeake_furthRdg2.htm.

Not only did head rights allow already prosperous men to increase their land holdings, they rapidly increased the number of indentured servants in the colonies. As an example, close to seventy-five percent of English settlers arriving in Virginia in the 1600s were indentured servants.[13] When the influx of indentured servants declined, head rights were extended to cover other laborers. The first group pulled into this system was British convicts who were bound laborers for seven years. When the supply of laborers from this group was depleted, head rights were extended to include imported slaves, which added an impetus toward a slave system.[14] Although other political[15] and economic[16, 17] advantages shifted the use of European indentured servants to the use of African slaves, reliance upon indentured servants lasted for a considerable time in the colonies.

---

13. For this and other statistical information, see the Virginia Historical Society's web site: http://www.vahistorical.org/sva2003/comparisonmassva.htm.

14. Interestingly, when the prohibitions against slavery became strong, reverse incentives in the form of taxes were added to the cost of each African brought to the American shore. An example of this can be seen in James Madison's comments in The Founders' Constitution: Volume 3, Article 1, Section 9, Clause 1, Document 16. (William T. Hutchinson et al. *The Papers of James Madison.* Chicago, U of Chicago P. The earliest instances of such taxation, however, have less to do with the inhumanity of the system than it does with the colonies concerns about the safety of its European citizens. As the ratio of black to white inhabitants began to favor black residents, colonies such as Virginia attempted to thwart the slave trade.

15. The influx of indentured servants to the colonies began to subside for various reasons: in Europe, the economic situation improved and the unemployment rate dropped dramatically. Furthermore, rumors of ill-treatment of servants who had gone to the colonies reached the European shores. For further detail, see Galenson David W 'The Rise and Fall of Indentured Servitude in the Americas: An Economic Analysis' (1984) 44.1 *The Journal of Economic History* 1.

16. The slave trade itself opened up in various ways. The monopolies were broken, and slaves became available from various European sources. Rhode Island and Massachusetts began to participate in the importation of Africans to the colonies.

17. The use of Africans was seen as advantageous because of physical and cultural realties. Beyond physical markers, the language barrier also aided the owners in recapturing runaways. Because many African tribes were disseminated throughout the colonies, communication was difficult if not impossible for the new arrivals. This increased the possibility of recapturing any individual who fled, but more importantly, it dissuaded individuals from running in the first place. Finally, the geography and climate of the colonies were new to the Africans, which also functioned as a preventative for escape. The new arrivals would have had no notion of where to run, or how to return to their homeland. See Galenson, David W. "White Servitude and the Growth of Black Slavery in Colonial America." *The Journal of Economic History* 41:1(1981). 39.

The indentured servants were contracted workers. They agreed to a set period of labor time during which their freedoms were limited and their labor was owned by their masters. The stipulations of the indentured servant contract lead to the development of slave codes. For example, an indentured servant promised his or her time, a period of years, rather than a particular product or skill. During this phase, the servant's time was owned, closely approximating the later development where the servants themselves would be owned. Also, throughout the terms of the contract, indentured servants were prohibited from marriage and reproduction. In cases where servants did marry, or women became encumbered by unwanted pregnancy, time would be added to the service contract. This would compensate the contract owner for any time or labor loss due to a servant's family obligations, physical incapacity, or resultant illness. These specific controls on marriage and reproduction were echoed in the later manifestations of slave codes.

Prior to the formalization of slavery in the colonies, the earliest Africans arriving at Jamestown[18] were subsumed into the indenture system. These first Africans disembarked at the Virginia Colony in 1620. Like the slaves who would later pour into the country by the thousands, these 20 were sold at auction. The distinction between what happened to these people and what would happen to those who followed was based upon the laws enacted in the interim. These people were auctioned, but it was their labor, not their person that was owned. Just like those on an indentured servant contract, these individuals were not lifetime slaves.

Although these people were taken to the colonies involuntarily, they were seemingly held responsible for the cost of their passage. It is unclear, however, what length of time they owed their master to cover the expense. Equally unclear was what working skills the early Africans had to offer outside of manual labor. Indentured servants' contracts ran anywhere from three to seven years, depending on their skill level: a skilled worker would receive a shorter contract than an unskilled laborer. The comparatively long indenture contract[19] given to the early African servants may reflect the workloads they were able to maintain in addition to the transport fees

---

18. It has long been suggested that the first slaves arrived on a Dutch warship coming from the Caribbean. A team of researchers, however, has recently claimed (2006) that the Africans were captured off a Portuguese slaving ship by British pirates. See Rein Lisa 'Mystery of Va.'s First Slaves Is Unlocked 400 Years Later' Washington *Post* 3 September 2006 p. A01.

19. The exact number of years of these contracts have been debated, but it seems that these individuals all received contracts much longer than the traditional indenture.

charged. Not surprisingly, female indentured servants functioned in domestic roles, were considered unskilled workers, and given longer contracts than their male counterparts. The first Africans were most likely assessed as unskilled laborers and given long-term contracts. Unfortunately, there were no records firmly establishing the terms for the first Africans, male or female, brought to the colonies. There are no early narratives written by these workers, due partially, no doubt, to language barriers. It is known, however, that many functioned under written contracts with time limitations. The precedent had been established by the large numbers of European workers functioning under similar contracts. When the Africans were released, like the indentured servants, they became free workers able to establish their own business ventures and take on indentured servants of their own.[20, 21] There are records of several Africans[22] who followed this blueprint and became rich land owners with hundreds of servants in their debt. This racially egalitarian servant system was, however, short-lived.

In rapid succession, a series of laws was enacted that defined servants as something quite different from slaves. Within these laws, issues of race, religion, and the definition of humanity become paramount. And, al-

---

20. In 1676, a black indentured servant named Thomas Hagleton took his master Thomas Truman, the owner of his indenture, to courts and won his freedom (Proceedings of the Provincial Court, 1675–1677. Archives of Maryland Online. http://www.archivesofmaryland.net/html/index.html).

21. With time, laws were instituted to prohibit Africans as well as Native Americans and Jews from holding contracts for Christians. For example, one act reads 'for a further christian care and usage of all christian servants, Be it also enacted, by the authority aforesaid, and it is hereby enacted, That no negros, mulattos, or Indians, although christians, or Jews, Moors, Mahometans, or other infidels, shall, at any time, purchase any christian servant, nor any other, except of their own complexion, or such as are declared slaves by this act: And if any negro, mulatto, or Indian, Jew, Moor, Mahometan, or other infidel, or such as are declared slaves by this act, shall, notwithstanding, purchase any christian white servant, the said servant shall, ipso facto, become free and acquit from any service then due, and shall be so held, deemed, and taken: And if any person, having such christian servant, shall intermarry with any such negro, mulatto, or Indian, Jew, Moor, Mahometan, or other infidel, every christian white servant of every such person so intermarrying, shall, ipso facto, become free and acquit from any service then due to such master or mistress so intermarrying, as aforesaid.' Act XI: An Act Concerning Servants and Slaves. 3 Hening (VA) 447 (OCT. 1705).

22. One example, presented in the WGBS documentary *Africans in America: America's Journey Through Slavery*, is that of 'Antonio the negro,' who changed his name to Anthony Johnson gained his freedom, and he soon owned land and cattle and even indentured servants of his own.

though there was most definitely life-long servitude earlier in the colonies, the Act of 1655[23] was one of the first legislated documents to utilize the term slavery, in this case in reference to Indian slavery. Various terms were used to differentiate the indentured servants fulfilling term contracts from those who would later be called slaves. The terms "servant for life," "perpetual servant" and "bond servant" were used interchangeably with 'slave'... and the servant who became slave lost all the earmarks of a servant.'[24] As the expansion of slavery encompassed the colonies, parallel systems of servitude were maintained. These included both white and black indentured servants. With time, the system of black indenture faded and the codification of slavery moved steadily forward.

One of the first ways in which this shift can be traced is through the Virginia Act of 1662, quoted above: it was a momentous piece of legislation because it removed any ambiguity about the status of mulatto children born of slave mothers. The slave status, now inherited through the mother, disqualified any privilege that could have been inherited through the father. This condemned children born of free black men as well as those fathered by white men. Although privilege was certainly granted to slaves with lighter pigmentation, this was a custom based upon the developing racist attitudes in the colonies rather than a legal right. The Act was significant also because it was one of the first colonial American shifts away from English Common Law, in which inheritance and class status were tracked through the paternal line.

Not inconsequentially, the Act also enabled a variety of abuses: the primary repercussion was that slave women were increasingly vulnerable to rape by their owners, overseers, and other free men. No longer would the children of such unions present economic or legal hardships for the fathers who engendered them. Instead, the children would be assets rather than potential drains in a financial ledger. The passage of this Act provided the slave owner with a means to increase his slave property, an

---

23. ACT I. An Induction to the Acts concerning Indians. 1 Hening (VA) 369 (Mar. 1655): 'If the Indians shall bring in any children as gages of their good and quiet intentions to us and amity with us, then the parents of such children shall choose the persons to whom the care of such children shall be intrusted and the countrey by us their representatives do engage that wee will not use them as slaves, but do their best to bring them up in Christianity, civillity and the knowledge of necessary trades; And on the report of the commissioners of each respective country that those under whose tuition they are, do really intend the bettering of the children in these particulars then a salary shall be allowed to such men as shall deserve and require it.'

24. Davis, 261.

issue of increasing significance after the prohibition of slave importation in 1808.

Although slaves were still smuggled into the country as contraband, the easier route to increase human property was the forced pregnancy of existing slave women. This came in the form of coerced sexual activity between slaves or the rape of enslaved women by their owners. Of course, not all sexual interactions between masters and slaves were acts of rape,[25] as evidenced by marriage records of such unions and anecdotal material discussing love relationships between master and slave. However, the majority of children born of a master and slave relationship were extramarital activities on the part of the master regardless of the emotional or familial attachments of the slave women. Laws were enacted to prevent such marriages between masters/mistresses and their slaves: at first, the prohibitions came in the form of financial and social penalties but evolved into legislation banning them entirely. The cost of breaking these laws ranged from large financial fines to banishment. Laws were later enacted against any clergy member who performed wedding ceremonies between slaves and their owners.

In relation to the children born of such unions there came a second, perhaps unforeseen, repercussion: the inevitable shift in the use of physical features to designate race. As the rape of slave women by European-ancestored men was replicated in subsequent generations, the designation of African or black became an ambiguous reference. Although cultures like that of Cuba had an enormously detailed system to define one's class status dependent upon racial mixing,[26] the United States did not develop such detailed codification. The lack of codification based upon minute racial distinctions seems like it should have led to liberal treatment of individuals who blurred racial lines. But, instead, it developed into a blanket categorization ultimately becoming the "one-drop rule"[27] used to designate

---

25. It is important to note the problematic scenario of marriage and concubinage between a slave owner and his current or emancipated slave. The power dynamics dictated that seemingly consensual sex remained acts of violence.

26. 'In colonial Spanish America, civil rights and responsibilities were based directly on the degree of European blood that a person had. Consequently, racial classifications were highly elaborated, and minor distinctions in ancestry were carefully recorded' www.tarver-genealogy.net. See attached chart for a demonstration of the minute distinctions. For images that accompanied these categorizations, visit the website: http://www.tarver-genealogy.net/visual/exhibits/castas/ulthm1_6.html.

27. The one-drop rule was the standard used to define an individual as 'colored.' The rule was significant for the post war years, and connected to issues of intermarriage and 'Jim Crow Laws.'

race. This stated that if there were but one drop of black blood coursing through an individual's veins, then that person was black and enslaved.[28]

Once such a law became established in one colony, depending upon its economic and social usefulness, it would then spread to the other colonies. So, the laws established by Virginia were replicated by various other colonies, and the features of slavery became recognized and institutionalized throughout the land. For example, the Virginia Act of 1705,[29] which established the definition of slaves as chattel, was quickly adopted. Although the system had functioned on this premise, it was now codified in law. The vestiges of the servant status held by the first Africans evaporated. The ramification of this one linguistic and legal change was dramatic. The people held in slavery were now on a par with property, livestock, and legally opened to inhuman treatment.

Falling upon the heels of the 1662 precedent established by Virginia was the law approved by the Assembly of Maryland in 1664.[30] In this act, Maryland defined slavery as a permanent condition and further entrenched the definition of slaves in a race based system. Not only did it stipulate that all Negroes brought to the colony would be slaves, it expressly defined all Negroes existing in the colony as slaves. This law cemented their status, removing any slippage caused by the earlier structure of black indenture. Other aspects of this law were race based: where once "children of white mothers and slave fathers became servants for a term of years,"[31] this act specified that all children of enslaved men would be slaves for life as would any children of free women and enslaved men: "For deterring such free borne women from such shamefull Matches ... whatsoever free

---

28. *In Life and Times of Frederick Douglass*, Douglass detailed it this way:

'Slavery had no recognition of fathers, as none of families. That the mother was a slave was enough for its deadly purpose. By its law the child followed the condition of its mother. The father might be a freeman and the child a slave. The father might be a white man, glorying in the purity of his Anglo-Saxon blood, and his child ranked with the blackest slaves. Father he might be, and not be husband, and could sell his own child without incurring reproach, if in its veins coursed one drop of African blood' in Douglass, Frederick *Life And Times Of Frederick Douglass: His Early Life As A Slave, His Escape From Bondage, And His Complete History: An Autobiography.* Gramercy Books, New York, 1993. 3.

29. 3 Hening (VA) 333 (Oct. 1705).

30. Assembly Proceedings (MD) 533 (Sept. 1664).

31. Davis T R 'Negro Servitude in the United States: Servitude Distinguished from Slavery' (1923)8 *The Journal of Negro History* 247–83. 263.

borne woman shall inter marry with any slave … shall Serve the master of such slave dureing the life of her husband And that all the issue of such free-borne woemen soe marryed shall be Slaves as their fathers were" [Original spelling retained].[32] A grandfather clause stipulated that children of a free woman and a slave born before passage of the law would be bound to 30 years of service. Now, any free woman who married a slave would be bound to servitude for the lifetime of her husband.

This particular provision shifted back and forth: the case of Irish Nell,[33] a white woman whose husband was a slave, became a sticking point. Not only did this law conflict with that of Virginia, but the idea that a white woman would be bound to slavery also drew public complaint. Clearly, the initial stipulation was aimed at free black or Indian women who married slaves. Another ramification of the difference between the laws of Virginia and those of Maryland "inspired mass flight between the two colonies. Interracial families headed by African men and European women fled from Maryland to Virginia, while those headed by African women and European men ran away from Virginia to Maryland."[34] Additionally, it was found that "Maryland planters, with a view towards breeding additional human assets, were exploiting the law by deliberately 'purchasing white women' and forcing them to wed African men."[35] In order to curb this, Maryland augmented this portion of its law to match the inheritance procedures of Virginia. However, through this act, slavery became synonymous with blackness, and legislation prohibiting interracial marriage was ratified. Other colonies soon followed Maryland's "anti-amalgamation" laws. In 1691, a Virginia law declared that any white man or woman who married a "Negro, mulatto, or Indian" would be banished from the colony forever[36] and later laws included increasingly harsh pun-

32. Catterall Helen Tunnicliff and James J Hayden *Judicial Cases Concerning American Slavery and the Negro* Octagon Books. New York. 1968.

33. Diggs Ellen Irene *Black Chronology from 4000 B C to the Abolition of the Slave Trade* Hall Boston 1983. Diggs points out that 'Planters sometimes married white women servants to Blacks in order to transform these servants and their children into slaves.'

34. Sweet Frank W 'The Invention of the Color Line: 1691 '06 April 2006 see http://backintyme com/essay050101.htm.

35. Sweet Frank W.

36. *Africans in America: America's Journey Through Slavery.* Dirs. Orlando Bagwell Susan Bellows.

ishments "for anyone complicit in a crime of intermarriage, up to and including death by torture."[37]

The human experiences behind each law, indeed, each sub-section of these laws, impelled people to share their lives in writing. Frederick Douglas, despite being a champion of all enslaved people, decried his situation as mulatto, and his work highlighted the awkwardness, if not absurdity, of racial categorization. Harriet Jacobs' story of her treatment by her master focused upon the vulnerability of slave women to sexual exploitation and abuse. Both responded to the definition of slaves as chattel. These are only two examples of the multitudes of individuals who suffered under the developments of American slave codes. They were the fortunate ones who escaped from slavery and were privileged enough to have access to both language and economic support allowing them to tell their tales.

---

37. Guild June Purcell Black *Laws of Virginia; a Summary of the Legislative Acts of Virginia Concerning Negroes from Earliest Times to the Present Negro* Universities Press New York 1969 p. 86.

Chapter Two

Reflections of Law in Slave Narratives/Slave Narratives Influencing the Law[1]

In order to discuss American slave law, two powerful voices have been selected to speak for the millions that were silenced: Frederick Douglass and Harriet Jacobs. Each of these writers utilized their life experiences for the benefit of the abolitionist movement. By exploring their writing, the ramifications of legal precedents take on a human face, a voice of protest, and draw attention to the dehumanizing aspects of the legal shifts in colonial laws.

Frederick Douglass was perhaps the most famous spokesperson of his age. Although figures like Harriet Tubman,[2] the celebrated organizer of the Underground Railroad, were responsible for providing concrete personal help for enslaved people, it was Douglass who gained national prominence as a political influence. He was most celebrated for his slave narrative although equally important were his public speaking engagements and his involvement in the publication of the *North Star*, the abolitionist newspaper. Due to these publications, and his national tours as a spokesperson for the American Anti-Slavery Society, Douglass engaged the nation in the

---

1. *Portions of this chapter have been reprinted with generous permission of* The Australian Feminist Law Journal. *See Hendrick, Veronica.* Colonial American Slave Laws: Frederick Douglass and Harriet Jacobs Highlight Consequences for Slave Women. (2006)*25 Australian Feminist Law Journal* 41–59.

2. Tubman's activities developed a clandestine machine, which enabled runaway slaves to journey from the southern slave states to the free states in the North. The operation was an elaborate network of abolitionists located in both regions of the nation. Slaves were aided in their escape, and upon arrival in the North, they were provided with various resources to ensure the continuation of their liberty: housing, work, and most importantly, false documentation proving their free status. For a detailed discussion of the Tubman's role in the Underground Railroad, see Okur Nilgun Anadolu 'Underground Railroad in Philadelphia, 1830–1860' (1995)*25.5 Journal of Black Studies* 537.

debate over slavery. Even after the Civil War and the Emancipation Proclamation of 1863,[3] Douglass continued to fight against oppression. He was involved in the fight for voting rights and other civil liberties of freed blacks and was instrumental in the women's movement. However, for the purpose of this discussion, focus remains upon his autobiographical work which highlights his anguish as a slave.

Douglass' 1845 narrative began with statements about his birth, a common trope of autobiography. Much like the opening of a Dickens novel, Douglass listed the place he was born and the name of his mother. Yet, in this opening page Douglass presented two specifics, both of which were unprovable because of his status as a slave: the first was his birth date and the second was the name of his father. Douglass was only able to approximate his age, stating that "by far the larger part of the slaves know as little of their ages as horses know of theirs."[4] As to his father, all he was able to offer was "My father was a white man. He was admitted to be such by all I ever heard speak of my parentage. The opinion was also whispered that my master was my father; but of the correctness of this opinion, I know nothing; the means of knowing was withheld from me."[5] Douglass then commented on the distant relationship he had with his mother, whom he saw on rare occasions and who died when he was just seven. With this opening, a human response to the inhuman laws of slavery was presented.

The fact that Douglass did not know his birth date may seem inconsequential until he equated this ignorance with the senselessness of a horse. Douglass scrutinized his animal status through analysis of his parentage. Importantly, his mother, Harriet Bailey, was described as a dark skinned

---

3. Lincoln, Abraham. *Speeches And Writings, 1859–1865: Speeches, Letters, And Miscellaneous Writings, Presidential Messages And Proclamations* New York Viking Press 1989 p 438. *The Emancipation Proclamation*: 'That on the 1st day of January, A.D. 1863, all persons held as slaves within any State or designated part of a State the people whereof shall then be in rebellion against the United States shall be then, thenceforward, and forever free; and the executive government of the United States, including the military and naval authority thereof, will recognize and maintain the freedom of such persons and will do no act or acts to repress such persons, or any of them, in any efforts they may make for their actual freedom.' See also Lincoln Abraham 'The Emancipation Proclamation' *National Archives and Records Administration* 1863 see http://www.archives.gov/exhibits/featured_documents/emancipation_proclamation/transcript.html.

4. Douglass, Frederick. *Narrative of the Life of Frederick Douglass an American Slave* Anchor Press New York 1973.

5. Douglass, 3.

woman, darker than her own parents, whereas Douglass describes himself with anglo features and light skin. This may have been enough to conclude there was miscegenation in his conception, but Douglass has further detail. He stated that his mother's owner, Aaron Anthony, was the white man rumored to be his father. Several things became significant with this revelation. The first issue for Douglass was that his father treated him on a par with the other chattel on his land. For example, Douglass was removed from his mother before he was one-year old, which he explained was a common practice to eradicate human attachments between mother and child. Although he encountered his brother Perry and sister Eliza when he was moved to the Lloyd Plantation at the age of six, he had no emotional bonds with them. His familial bonds had been broken by his constant relocation, and the grandparents who raised him until he was six became distant figures. At this tender age, he had been broken of human attachments and was treated as livestock.

The second aspect of his parentage was the circumstances of his conception. His mother lived on property separate from the Anthony compound, yet she had, to our knowledge, three children by Anthony. The chances that these encounters stemmed out of a love relationship were small. The assumption was that Anthony used his slave, Harriet, for both physical pleasure and economic gain. The children she produced become his property, slaves that he could use to expand his holdings or sell if the situation called for it. With this came an awareness of Harriet Bailey's own life, which was short and seemingly filled with sorrow. She was separated from her parents and put to labor in an isolated location. Although the slave communities were familiar with the constant shift in membership, the experience of integrating into a new environment was no easy task. Added to this, each of Harriet's children remained with her for only a year, just time enough to nurse them though infancy. When a child was removed, she would once again become pregnant, as evidenced in the close proximity in her children's ages. This indicated that Harriet was repeatedly approached by her master. She would have had no legal protection from his advances; in fact, the laws of the land facilitated such activity.

The sexual abuse of Harriet led to a twofold problem for Douglass himself. The first issue was his slave status, inherited from his mother, and the second issue related to his biracial designation. Upon Harriet's death, Douglass presented his situation this way:

> [My mother] left me without the slightest intimation of who my
> father was. The whisper that my master was my father, may or

may not be true; and, true or false, it is of but little consequence to my purpose whilst the fact remains, in all its glaring odiousness, that slaveholders have ordained, *and by law established, that the children of slave women shall in all cases follow the condition of their mothers*; and this is done too obviously to administer to their own lusts, and make a gratification of their wicked desires profitable as well as pleasurable; for by this cunning arrangement, the slaveholder, in cases not a few, sustains to his slaves the double relation of master and father [italics mine].[6]

As Douglass pointed to the legal framework allowing Harriet's abuse, the anger behind his words was self-evident. Not only did he highlight the suffering women experience at the hands of their masters, Douglass also explained other unfortunate ramifications of slave women bearing their masters' children: the harsh treatment they received from the master's wife. Douglass explained that these slave women were "a constant offence to their mistress. She is ever disposed to find fault with them; they can seldom do anything to please her; she is never better pleased than when she sees them under the lash."[7] Beyond his sympathy for the woman who bore him, and all women in her situation, Douglass' response revealed his personal sentiments.

Since he was the child of a white man—a man he knew and worked for—the conditions of his slavery had unique emotional underpinnings. The resentment he felt towards his owner/father was heightened with the awareness that he received no special treatment and no parental acknowledgement. Harriet's children, like the other slaves on the Lloyd Plantation, lived in squalor. Douglass describes his physical treatment in animal terms, being fed at a trough and huddling for warmth like beasts in a stable.

As further evidence of his status as chattel, Douglass highlighted the various exchanges of his person made in his life prior to his escape. Although he was only sold once, he was continually given in service to one family member or another. When his owner died, he became a matter of inheritance and was once again moved from his home. Douglass outlined the different working conditions he contended with while being owned by one master and lent out or rented to another. Through this detailing, Douglass outlined his status as property and railed against the institution of slav-

---

6. Douglass, 5.
7. Douglass, 5.

ery. Although his words were written as an escaped slave living in protected freedom in the North, under an assumed name, of course—his birth name was Frederick Augustus Washington Bailey—most of the situations of which he wrote were universal conditions faced by all slaves. His discussion focused not only upon the laws that defined slavery, but also upon some of the justifications behind these laws.

Of particular interest were Douglass' comments about the religiously based commentaries and maneuvers rationalizing the legal bondage of Africans. When the slave system was first allowed by Queen Elizabeth I, the spiritual and moral improvements of the Africans were offered as justification for their enslavement. The argument acknowledged that slavery was a deplorable condition but reasoned that the slaves would be enhanced through their exposure to Christianity. The definition of Africans as pagans, as savages, became entrenched in the slave system. However, when significant numbers of slaves wished to be freed based upon their conversion to Christianity, laws were enacted to prevent their release. The Virginia Act of 1667[8] stipulates that baptism would no longer free an enslaved person: "It is enacted and declared by this grand assembly and the authority thereof, that the conferring of baptisme doth not alter the condition of the person as to his bondage or ffreedome" [original spelling retained]. Although this Act neatly removed the ability of converted slaves to obtain their freedom based upon their Christianity, it also removed the justification for enslaving the "pagans" in the first place. Therefore, a new religiously-based rationalization was developed, and Cotton Mather[9] delineated its biblical foundation: in his *Rules for the Society of the Negroes*, written in 1693, Mather explained that "Negroes were enslaved because they had sinned against God." Now the designation of black races as the "sons of Ham" doomed by Noah to be "hewers of wood and drawers of water" became the rationale for black slavery and for its hereditary nature.[10]

Douglass addressed this point directly, connecting it to the mixed-raced slaves, such as himself, saying, "a very different-looking class of people are springing up at the south, and are now held in slavery" and it "will do away the force of the argument, that God cursed Ham, and therefore American slavery is right."[11] He further explained that "if the lineal descendants

---

8. 2 Hening (Va.) 195 (Sept. 1667).

9. Cotton Mather, the Puritan minister of Boston's Old North church, is most famous for his writings on witchcraft and influence on the Salem Witch Trials.

10. Ahluwalia Pal 'Race' (2006)23 *Theory Culture & Society* 538–545.

11. Douglass, 6.

of Ham are alone to be scripturally enslaved, it is certain that slavery at the south must soon become unscriptural; for thousands are ushered into the world, annually, who, like myself, owe their existence to white fathers."[12] In this narrative Douglass criticized the three most powerful laws of slavery: Virginia 1662-ACT XII, in which children followed the free or slave status of their mothers, the Maryland 1664 act which established slavery as a lifelong status, and the Virginia 1705 act which defined slaves to be legally regarded as real estate. Through Douglass' words, his experiences as a victim of these laws became part of the public consciousness leading up to the Civil War. Douglass' activities as both a spokesperson and writer empowered the abolitionist movement.

In like vein, the work of Harriet Jacobs was used to inflame public opinion. In the opening to her work, she pardoned herself for relating indelicate details of her life in slavery. She explained her motivation, stating: "I do this for the sake of my sisters in bondage, who are suffering wrongs so foul, that our ears are too delicate to listen to them. I do it with the hope of arousing conscientious and reflecting women at the North to a sense of their duty in the exertion of moral influence on the question of Slavery."[13] In this endeavor, Jacobs was highly successful. As already noted in Douglass' account, the suffering of women at the hands of their masters was a uniquely painful experience. Because Jacobs' writing focused upon her experiences as a woman in slavery, and focused particularly on the issue of sexual abuse, she was embraced. The women of the North were indeed provoked by her suffering, and they redoubled their efforts to liberate enslaved women.

Harriet Ann Jacobs, like Douglass, took a fake name to protect her from recapture once she arrived in the free North. Under the pen name Linda Brent, Jacobs wrote her 1860 autobiography titled *Incidents in the Life of a Slave Girl, Written by Herself*, and published in 1862 in England under the title *The Deeper Wrong*. In this work, Jacobs detailed her experiences of sexual abuse at the hands of her owner. Although there were moral prohibitions against fornication with slaves, libidinal desires and the economic pressures of the early 1800s won out. At the time of Jacobs' birth, the United States was embroiled in various discussions about the appropriateness of slavery. The topic of slavery had, in fact, been included in the deliberations at the Constitutional Congress in 1787. Section 9 of Article

---

12. Douglass, 6.
13. Jacobs, Harriet. *Incidents in the Life of a Slave Girl: Written by Herself* Harvard University Press Cambridge 1987.

I of the Constitution, in an effort to minimize the obvious tension between the northern and southern states, stipulated that prohibitions against the importation of slaves could not be considered before 1808, stating:

> The Migration or Importation of such Persons as any of the States now existing shall think proper to admit, shall not be prohibited by the Congress prior to the Year one thousand eight hundred and eight, but a Tax or duty may be imposed on such Importation, not exceeding ten dollars for each Person.[14]

Although this extended the slave trade into the 19th century, restrictions and prohibitions, such as taxes, made the slave trade increasingly problematic. In 1807, the law disallowing the importation of Africans was brought to the congressional table and ratified. It read:

> Be it enacted by the Senate and House of Representatives of the United States of America in Congress assembled, That from and after the first day of January, one thousand eight hundred and eight, it shall not be lawful to import or bring into the United States or the territories thereof from any foreign kingdom, place, or country, any negro, mulatto, or person of colour, with intent to hold, sell, or dispose of such negro, mulatto, or person of colour, as a slave, or to be held to service or labour.[Original spelling retained.][15]

Therefore, by 1808, the importation of American slaves became an illegal activity. Although this alteration was a moral victory with tangible results for potential new slaves, the condition of slaves already held in bondage was disregarded.

The ramifications of this action, coupled with the laws defining slavery as an inherited quality, facilitated sexual abuse throughout the country. Once slaves could no longer be imported, the obvious method for increasing the slave population was to force reproduction. The eugenic quality that had existed in the slave system, in which the strongest males were partnered with multiple women, became increasingly prevalent. Insuring such unions, however, was not always possible. As an expedient, the over-

---

14. The Founders' Constitution. Art. 1 Sec. 9, Cl. 1. http://press-pubs.uchicago.edu/founders/help/about.html.

15. An Act to Prohibit the Importation of Slaves into any Port or Place Within the Jurisdiction of the United States, From and After the First Day of January, in the Year of our Lord One Thousand Eight Hundred and Eight: U.S. Const. art. I, §1, 1807.

seers and masters took the liberty of performing insemination themselves. In the experiences retold by Jacobs, it was, however, evident that the motivations for acts of rape were not economically inspired. Through her writing, the cold acts inspired by law become vibrant human events.

Early in her narrative, Jacobs poignantly stated, "[I] never dreamed I was a piece of merchandise."[16] She recounted the shock she received upon discovering that her condition as a slave meant that she was property, legislated to be bought and sold. As evidence of this status, Jacobs recounted the hardships her family suffered trying either to prevent family members from being sold or to repurchase them once they had been auctioned. One instance was the plight of Jacobs' grandmother, who labored endlessly to purchase her children. Eventually the grandmother accumulated a vast sum of money, three hundred dollars, through the sale of her baked goods. However, when she told her mistress of her plans, the "mistress one day begged [the entire amount] as a loan, promising to pay her soon."[17] Jacobs emphasized the power of law in her narrative, stating that "the reader probably knows that no promise or writing given to a slave is legally binding; for, according to Southern laws, a slave, 'being' property, can 'hold' no property."[18] Needless to say, the grandmother had no recourse when the funds were not returned.

Jacobs conveyed earlier injustices perpetrated on her grandmother, Marthy, which specifically highlighted the sorrow of slave mothers. When Marthy's daughter—Jacobs' mother—was only three-months old, Marthy was forced to wean her own daughter in order to feed a baby white girl. When this white girl grew up, she inherited the children of her nurse, and when that same white girl died in adulthood, all the children of her nurse were relegated to the auction block. It was the death of this same white woman, the late Mrs. Horniblow, that engendered the horror of Jacobs' own young life. Yet, it was at the hands of her new owner, Dr. James Norcom,[19] that Jacobs learned the other laws governing slavery.

Jacobs told of her encounters with two women in his household who were impregnated by Norcom. The first woman was sold into slavery for naming him as the father of her child, and the other woman, really just a girl,

---

16. Jacobs, 5.
17. Jacobs, 6.
18. Jacobs, 6.
19. In the text, just as Jacobs changed her name to Linda Brent, the name of Norcom was changed to Flint. Jacobs used the pseudonyms Ellen and Benny Sands to refer to her own children, Louisa and Joseph Sawyer.

died in childbirth, her fair-skinned child following in short order. Jacobs' own victimization was recounted in her narrative, as was her abuse at the hands of her mistress. The earlier comments from Douglass' narrative are applicable here: a woman who was the unfortunate focus of her master's sexual attentions was made increasingly wretched through mistreatment by her resentful mistress. Therefore, Jacobs presented a twofold problem for Mrs. Norcom: Jacobs was adored by her charge, Mary, the mistress' daughter, and she was pursued by Norcom, the mistress' husband. Mary's fondness for Jacobs inspired Mrs. Norcom's petty cruelties, such as removing Jacobs' shoes and sending her on errands in the snow, but the attentions by Norcom himself motivated her mistress' more violent outbursts.

Despite the cruel treatment Jacobs received at the hands of her jealous mistress, Norcom did not relent in his pursuit. Jacobs relayed her revulsion after the first time she was sexually accosted by Norcom: "he told me that I was made for his use, made to obey his command in 'every' thing; that I was nothing but a slave, whose will must and should surrender to his."[20] She was delicate in her retelling, only setting up the scenario and explaining that she was "absorbed in painful reflections afterwards,"[21] but the events that transpired between the ellipses were quite clear. Norcom had used his privilege as a slave master to assault her without conscious or concern for reprisal.

Although Jacobs was able to repel her master from fully attaining his sexual goals, she was harassed by him for several years until she fled.[22] Jacobs spoke for all slave women when she stated that the "fifteenth year" was "a sad epoch in the life of a slave girl."[23] For the slave, beauty was a curse because "no matter whether the slave girl be as black as ebony or as fair as her mistress ... there is no shadow of law to protect her from insult, from violence, or even from death."[24] Jacobs not only noted the absence of protective laws, she emphasized the conditions of slavery which were protected by the legal structure: "the secrets of slavery are concealed like those

---

20. Jacobs, 18.
21. Jacobs, 18.
22. Although most readers take Jacobs' assertions about her ability to retain her chastity at face value, it may be implausible that Dr. Norcom would relent from crossing the final sexual barrier simply due to the threats Marthy made to his gentlemanly reputation. In fact, it becomes even more improbable given the fact that Jacobs meets several of Norcom other slaves who bear him children.
23. Jacobs, 27.
24. Jacobs, 27.

of the Inquisition. My master was, to my knowledge, the father of eleven slaves."[25] Speaking of such children, Jacobs explained that the fathers "regard such children as property, as marketable as the pigs on the plantation."[26] Here again, we have an ex-slave echoing the laws of slavery and utilizing the animal metaphor.

The final section in which Jacobs directly commented upon the laws of slavery came when she first falls in love with a neighboring man, a free black man. Her master disallowed her union with him: Norcom not only declined to sell Jacobs to her admirer, but also refused their union, and prevented any other association. Jacobs called attention to her inability as a slave to select her own partner, but more importantly she discussed the implications of her union, had it been allowed. When her dejected lover left the state, she felt a certain sense of relief because she knew what burdens she would have presented as a wife of a free man. He would have been unable to protect her from the abuses of her owners, and he would have been equally unable to protect his children:

> Even if he could have obtained permission to marry me while I was a slave, the marriage would give him no power to protect me from my master. It would have made him miserable to witness the insults I should have been subjected to. And then, if we had children, I knew they must 'follow the condition of the mother.'[27]

By expressly discussing the laws of slavery in her narrative, even quoting the Virginia law,[28] Jacobs enabled her work to become a tool of the abolitionist movement. Her key audience was the women of the North, whose activities helped build national momentum toward change.

American women had become dynamic in presenting their concerns to political representatives, and as time moved forward, their pleas took on the form of demands: "the rhetoric of female antislavery petitions and appeals [moved] from a tone of humility to a tone of insistence, reflected an ongoing transformation of the political identity."[29] The result of this shift was twofold: the women's unrelenting demand for the abolition of slavery added to the growing condemnation of the institution, and the results of

---

25. Jacobs, 35.
26. Jacobs, 36.
27. Jacobs, 42.
28. 2 Hening (Va.) 170 (Dec. 1862).
29. Zaeske, Susan. *Signatures of Citizenship: Petitioning Antislavery and Women's Political Identity.* U of North Carolina P: Chapel Hill, 2003: 12.

their actions—especially their ability to influence political action—in-spired desire for increased political participation and the expansion of the rights of women, specifically the right to vote.[30] Although women of the United States waited until 1920 to receive this right, their participation in the abolitionist movement was a resounding success. Without the voice of women such as Jacobs,[31] the process of emancipation would have been deferred.

Through the *Narrative of the Life of Frederick Douglass, an American Slave* and *Harriet Jacobs: Incidents in the Life of a Slave Girl* the laws of slavery come alive. Reading statutes and following the progression of acts and laws themselves lends insight to the period, but hearing the voices of the past shifts intellectual understanding into the realm of emotion. The impassioned speeches of both Douglass and Jacobs motivated the audiences who heard them, but it was their writing that inspired the nation. The plight of Douglass and Jacobs, as well as the stories of abused women embedded in their narratives, galvanized the anti-slavery societies in both the North and the South. These writers, and others like them, unearthed the hidden atrocities of the slave system and incensed the public. Without these emotional pressures, the slave system would have extended for decades because the abolition of slavery was dependent upon sentiment: the rules of justice had long been overthrown by the rules of economics.

---

30. Early on in the women's abolitionist movement, the battle for women suffrage was intertwined with the anti-slavery movement. However, as an expedient, the two issues were divided so that the greater of the two oppressions could be concluded. Champions of the abolitionist movement, such as Frederick Douglas, were also involved in the fight for women's rights, but moved away from the issues so as to focus upon the more readily attainable goal of slave liberation. The nineteenth amendment to the Constitution of the United States, which granted women the right to vote, was not ratified until 1920. See Quarles, Benjamin 'Frederick Douglass and the Woman's Rights Movement, (1940) 25 *The Journal of Negro History* 35.

31. An important woman's voice was that of Sojourner Truth. She, unlike Douglass and Jacobs, was a slave of a Northern state—New York. After escaping, Truth added her voice to the cry for freedom: Her most memorable speech titled 'Ain't I A Woman?' was delivered at the 1851 Women's Convention in Akron, Ohio. In it were these words:' I have borne thirteen children, and seen most all sold off to slavery, and when I cried out with my mother's grief, none but Jesus heard me!' See Gilbert, Olive. Sojourner Truth and Nell Irvin Painter *Narrative of Sojourner Truth: A Bondswoman of Olden Time with a History of Her Labors and Correspondence Drawn from Her Book of Life; also A Memorial Chapter* Penguin Books New York 1998.

Chapter Three

American Legacies: Slave Laws and Envisioned Lives

In the lead up to the US Civil War, various concessions were made among the states to keep the Union solvent. One of the most provocative instances was the 1850 Fugitive Slave Act that enabled the union to cohere for little more than a decade. Building upon the Fugitive Slave Act of 1793 and the federal case of Prigg v. Pennsylvania (1842)—which noted that the viability of early fugitive slave acts was undermined by free states that disallowed or inhibited the transport of recaptured slaves—the 1850 law heightened the rights of slave owners and increased the responsibility of free states to return runaway slaves. This new Act ensured that escaped slaves would be captured and transported across state borders, and it established various precedents which led to the erosion of slave rights in individual states. Embedded within the new law were provisions that forced all law officials, not just Federal Marshals, to participate in the recapture of a designated runaway or face a fine of $1000 dollars. In response to earlier state laws which demanded that accusations against a fugitive be verified in court, the 1850 Act recognized the sworn testimony of the claimant as evidence enough to support a runaway's conveyance South. Ancillary to the law itself were widespread abuses: black men and women, regardless of their status as slave, manumitted, or freeborn, were kidnapped and sold into slavery. American fiction, both contemporaneous with and posterior to the law and modern work, retells the terror invoked by the slave catcher. Harriet Beecher Stowe's *Uncle Tom's Cabin* and Toni Morrison's *Beloved* develop the choice of suicide/infanticide over that of the slave catcher, and Edward P. Jones' *The Known World* describes the multiple problems presented by conditions of the 1850 Act.

The writings of Morrison created historical settings in which slavery and its consequences can be traced and analyzed. The novels *Beloved* and *Song of Solomon* focused most directly on slavery and its aftermath; nonetheless, much of Morrison's fiction emphasized the conflicts generated by America's involvement in slavery. In response to this history, all of Morrison's characters dreamt of freedom in one form or another. The desire to escape, break, or erase the slave experience in *Beloved* was as strong as the desire to circumvent, supplant, or retaliate against the subsequent systems of white domination presented in *Song of Solomon*.

In *Beloved*, the slaves on the Sweet Home farm made great sacrifices to place themselves on free soil. The escape plan developed by the Sweet Home slaves was a simple one: run from the farm and meet up with the Underground Railroad, which would carry them north across the Mississippi and to the free state of Ohio. However, the escape went terribly wrong and each of the running slaves met with horrible retribution. The farm's overseer punished each slave in a unique way: Sethe was sexually abused, Halle was mentally destroyed, Paul D was physically humiliated, and Sixo was burnt alive. These punishments destroyed each slave's vision of freedom yet they were in keeping with the rights guaranteed to masters under the slave codes.

When the main character Sethe decided to run, she was nine months pregnant and had lived most of her adult life on the Sweet Home farm. Her decision to run, and that of the other slaves as well, was caused by the arrival of the new overseer, Schoolteacher. Although Sethe's work remained, for the most part, manageable, the male slaves began to suffer from brutal treatment. When all the runaway plans went wrong, Sethe was impelled to attempt the escape alone. Her motivation to flee was not limited to a reaction against the treatment she received as a slave; instead, she ran from a list that Schoolteacher made in which her animal and "humanish" characteristics were lined up on opposing sides of the page. This list, and the knowledge that her children would be assessed as animals, inspired her flight from the Sweet Home plantation. Prior to the arrival of Schoolteacher, the slaves' codification as property was obscure. With Schoolteacher's arrival, and the laws he enforced, the status of the Sweet Home slaves was quickly established as that of working chattel.

Under Mr. Garner, the original owner, the slaves had been treated as servants rather than slaves. There were no chains, no limits on food, and no beatings. Garner had allowed the men to carry guns and hire their time out for pay. In fact, Sethe's husband had purchased the freedom of his mother and had full intention to buy freedom for himself and his growing family. Although the slave codes of Mississippi allowed for this arrangement, Garner's overall treatment of his slaves irritated his fellow townsmen. The narrator indicated that Garner's unexpected death may have been a case of murder: one of the townsmen admonished Garner regarding his attitude towards his slaves, chastising him for refusing to stud the males and declining to sell off individuals to cover expenses. This townsman also accused Garner of criminal behavior by allowing the slaves to carry guns.

The illusion of their servant-like status was ripped away from the Sweet Home slaves upon Garner's death. The true nature of their situation was made clear when Schoolteacher arrived and brought with him the force of law. It is important to note that Sethe had certainly heard horror stories of other plantations and slave experiences, but she had dismissed them. Only later in the novel does Sethe remember her own life as a toddler and the severe atmosphere on a plantation where her mother was burned to death for attempting to run. Of the other five adult slaves on the Sweet Home farm, only two had been born elsewhere: one man was bought from a different farm and another man came directly from Africa.[1] Their isolation on Sweet Home may explain the shock felt by the slaves when their freedoms were cut and their codification as animals was established. The laws of slavery had come to Sweet Home with destructive force.

Along with the law that redefined the slaves as property came the cultural perspectives defining Africans and their descendants as subhuman. Sethe overheard Schoolteacher instructing his two nephews, who were studying the differentiation between blacks and whites. Using physiological features as evidence, the boys divided their notebooks and categorized the slaves' animal properties. The definition of Sethe as an animal, equated with livestock, was a pivotal point of the novel. Over and over, examples of Sethe's animal nature were emphasized, and it was precisely this definition of slave which Sethe rejected. Like the historical case of Margaret Garner,[2] on which Morrison's novel was based, Sethe chose infanticide and death rather than allow herself or her children to return to slavery.

On the night of the planned escape, Schoolteacher instructed his nephews to abuse Sethe, not knowing that her husband, Halle, was hiding in the loft of the barn as a silent witness. As the six-month pregnant Sethe was whipped and sexually assaulted by the adolescent boys, the overseer was quantifying her animal characteristics. Sethe's words indicated that the two actions

---

1. There is an historical incongruity in the character of Sixo, who is said to be an African. The importation of slaves ceased in 1808. Either Sixo had been imported as contraband or Morrison overlooked this detail.

2. January, 1856, Margaret Garner, a runaway Kentucky slave, and several of her companions were surrounded by US Marshals as they hid in a shed in the Free State of Ohio. Rather than return to slavery, Garner took a meat cleaver to her infant daughter and attempted to kill her other four children and herself before she was apprehended, imprisoned, and tried. Significantly, the crime for which she is convicted was not murder, but instead theft and destruction of property—her children.

were equally destructive: "Two boys with mossy teeth, one sucking on my breast the other holding me down, their book-reading teacher watching and writing it up." After this humiliation, which Sethe invoked time and time again with the chant-like refrain "they stole my milk," she was beaten. Importantly, the physical brutality which Sethe suffered, the lashing of her back, was not the destructive force that later in the novel pushed her to infanticide. Instead, the rupture of her self-perception as a wife and mother—as human—drove her action.

The removal of the respect and dignity with which the Sweet Home slaves had been treated and their redefinition to the legal status of real estate is what Morrison emphasizes. The environment created by the Garners inspired false perceptions for the slaves. The laws of slavery and the customs maintained in the deep south of Mississippi did not rule on the Sweet Home Farm under the Garners; in fact, several of the laws of slavery were flagrantly broken by the Garners. Sethe and Halle were allowed to marry and raise their family, Baby Suggs was allowed to read, the men were allowed to carry guns, and Halle was allowed possession of his own free time. After the death of Mr. Garner, and the arrival of Schoolteacher, Mrs. Garner's brother-in-law, that fantasy was shattered. The security of the family was destroyed as Sethe and Halle were separated, and the potential to buy their own freedom was removed entirely. Under Mr. Garner's rule, Halle had been allowed to rent himself out to neighboring farms on his free days. It was in this way that Halle was able to buy his mother's freedom.[3]

Also eradicated by the arrival of Schoolteacher was Halle's pride in his status as a man and his ability to care for his family. Witnessing Sethe's abuse and recognizing his inability to protect her and their children destroyed Halle's false claim to manhood and freedom. The rupture of this fantasy shattered Halle's mind. The last view of Halle comes from Paul D, one of the Sweet Home slaves who reappears in the novel after the close of the Civil War. Paul D retells his last encounter with Sethe's' husband, explaining

---

3. Baby Suggs indicates that Garner's kindness was somewhat suspect. She knew her monetary value was low, and she questioned the value of her freedom: "What does a sixty-odd-year-old slave woman who walks like a three-legged dog need freedom for" (Morrison 1987)? When Garner asked Suggs to verify that he was a good master because he allowed Halle to buy her, she answered, "Yes, sir, you did" but thought to herself, "you got my boy and I'm all broke down. You be renting him out to pay for me way after I'm gone to Glory" (Morrison 1987). Therefore, allowing Halle to work for Suggs' price—she is surely more valuable to Halle than to a slave trader—was not as kind as it first appeared.

that Halle was "squatting by the churn smearing the butter as well as its clabber all over his face because the milk they took [was] on his mind." Like Halle, Paul D's experiences on this ill-fated night destroyed his fantasy of manhood under the slavery system. Schoolteacher's response to Paul D's attempt to run came in the form of chains, an enormous iron collar, and a metal bit forced into his mouth. Paul D was transformed into a workhorse ready for sale.

Morrison reemphasized the power of law to define slaves as property through further comparisons between humans and animals. On Sweet Home, the move from man to slave happened overnight, and for Paul D this transformation was crystallized when he encountered a rooster sitting free while he was being marched off for sale. Retelling his life to Sethe twenty years after their separation, Paul D recalled thinking that the rooster named Mister had become more of a man than he was:

> Mister was allowed to be and stay what he was. But I wasn't allowed to be and stay what I was. Even if you cooked him you'd be cooking a rooster named Mister. But wasn't no way I'd ever be Paul D again, living or dead. Schoolteacher changed me. I was something else and that something was less than a chicken sitting in the sun on a tub.

The recognition of difference between the status of a human and that of an animal gave momentum to the novel and motivation for the characters. And it was through such moments of insight that Morrison's descriptions of slaves as property emphasized law.

In *Beloved*, the Kentucky codes of slavery of the 1860s were used to define the legal status of the Sweet Home slaves. Starting in the 1600s and continuing up until the 1860s, an extensive body of law developed around the status of slaves and the rights of the slave owner. Although every slave state had its own slave code and body of court decisions, the slave codes of all states "made slavery a permanent condition, inherited through the mother, and defined slaves as property."[4] Morrison used this information as well as the actual events of a runaway slave by the name of Margaret Garner to add an important dimension to her fiction. By "reenacting the anguish of Margaret Garner, the slave woman," Morrison linked her novel to American history of the slave system. The novel steps out of the role of literature and becomes a larger commentary on the American past. Steven Weisenburger retells the tale of the *Historical Margaret Garner*:

---

4. Slave Codes 1860.

On a snowy, bitter cold Monday morning in late-January, 1856, Margaret Garner and seven members of her family made a daring escape from their enslavement on two neighboring Kentucky plantations. After walking across the frozen Ohio River at Covington, Kentucky, the fugitives found temporary shelter on Cincinnati's west side, at the cabin of a free man of color named Joseph Kite. The Garner party sojourned no farther northward than that point. Pursuing federal Marshals and the slave master who claimed Margaret and her four children had surrounded Kite's cabin. The twenty-two year old mother of four made a fateful decision: rather than return to slavery she would take her children's lives, then her own. By the time deputies broke in and subdued her husband Robert, Margaret had killed her two-and-one-half year-old daughter Mary. One month later the Garners were remanded to their Kentucky masters, but only after the most lengthy and divisive fugitive slave process of the pre-Civil War decades.[5]

By creating the link between fiction and historical events, Morrison's novel took on the role of social commentary and connected to the slave narratives of Douglass and Jacobs. Through the various characters, the novel represented first the fantasy of freedom within the slave system and then emphasized how brutally the reality of the slave system eradicated such false hope.

Left out of the portion of Weisenburger's summary presented above was the fact that Margaret Garner was tried for her act of infanticide and found guilty.[6] The salient point was that her guilt was not the act of murder, but instead the destruction of property. Therefore the animal metaphor which Morrison used throughout her novel becomes that much more important. Sethe, the Margaret Garner character, fled from slavery because she could not allow her children to be weighed and measured like cattle. Paul D and Halle suffered because their manhood was ripped away and

---

5. A Historical Margaret Garner: Weisenburger's comments reflected the research he has done in his book Modern Medea: a family story of slavery and child-murder from the Old South. An interesting deviation was that the opera concludes with Margaret Garner's death. In the opera, she committed suicide. In the historical documentation, Margaret Garner drowned when the ship carrying her back to slavery founders.

6. The novel Beloved did explain that Sethe was tried for her act of infanticide, but that she escaped the return to the Sweet Home farm because she was useless as a slave. Again, animal imagery was used: Schoolteacher chastised his nephews for too brutally handling her, the way one can ruin the temperament of a horse.

they were reduced to creatures with a status less than a rooster. And Sixo, the slave who refused to accept his role as an animal, was killed.

Unlike the others on the Sweet Home farm, Sixo was emotionally outside of the restrictions the slave system tried to impose upon his self-perception. Throughout the novel, Sixo, who was described as "indigo with a flame-red tongue," never doubted his manhood. He did not need to fantasize about freedom, he remembered it. He was the only African on the farm whereas the rest had been born into slavery. And he was also the only one, prior to the attempted run, to break the few rules that did exist on Sweet Home. He secretly left the farm to meet "Patsy the Thirty-Mile Woman," with whom he conceived a child. Therefore, Sixo's reactions to the arrival of Schoolteacher were different from those of the other Sweet Home slaves. Unlike Sethe and Halle, who attempted to navigate the newly enforced laws of slavery, Sixo rejected the system entirely. Sixo gave up learning first numbers and then the language of his American owners. Paul D explained that Sixo saw "no future in it" and when Schoolteacher "commenced to carry round a notebook and write down what we said ... it was them questions that tore Sixo up. Tore him up for all time." What "tore him up" was the audacity of the questions posed to evaluate his human and animal features. Sixo rejected this codification and joined with the others in the attempt to escape from the control of the new overseer. Sixo's reaction to his recapture also differed from that of the other slaves because he refused to be broken under torture and refused to capitulate to Schoolteacher's requests. Even as Sixo was being slowly burnt to death, he was able to shout out "Seven-O! Seven-O!" in honor of the child Thirty-Mile Woman was carrying in her womb. With his death, the power of Schoolteacher and the laws of slavery were concretized.

Sethe was the only other Sweet Home slave who remained unbroken. In fact, just like Sixo, the methods Schoolteacher used to break her only solidified her resolve. Also like Sixo, it was Schoolteacher's questions and their application to her children that convinced Sethe to run because "no one, no body on this earth, would list her daughter's characteristics on the animal side of the paper." Despite her swollen belly and weeping back, despite the fact that all the runaway plans had gone awry, despite the fact that the Underground Railroad had left without her and she could not find her husband and the other men had been caught, despite all of these mishaps, Sethe's newly conceived understanding of the laws of slavery impelled her desperate flight.

Once Sethe was firmly ensconced in a small house in Free Ohio, living with her mother-in-law, Baby Suggs, she experienced fulfillment of the fantasy created by the Garners. She embraced freedom and motherhood and claimed her humanity. All four of her children surrounded her. The two sons and young daughter she had sent ahead through the Underground Railroad were all in good health when Sethe arrived. With her Sethe brought her infant daughter, Denver, who was prematurely born during Sethe's flight from Sweet Home. The successful birth of Denver was enabled by her namesake, Amy Denver, a white indentured servant. Amy was most likely also a runaway, which provides a unique intersection between the laws covering both servant and slaves.

Morrison's brief use of Amy pulled into the text representations of other American codes of servitude.[7] Stemming out of the British system of indenture, the American system utilized and maintained voluntary bound service far after its dissolution in Great Britain. Alexa Silver Cawley explained the thin line between slaves and indentured servants: "indentured servants lived in a status of half-freedom. While legally considered chattel, like other forms of property…, a servant's potential labor rather than their persons belonged to the master."[8] The difference between the slaves and indentured servants had two significant features. The primary point was the above mentioned issue of self-ownership from which the second significant difference arose, that of voluntary enlistment. The very fact that servants entered into agreements, ostensibly of their own free will, coupled with term limits, created a chasm between the two groups. This difference was clearly perceived and acted upon by both Sethe and Amy.

Another feature of indenture was its application to only the contracted individual and its lack of heritability. Nonetheless, for Amy, the status of indenture was passed on to her by her mother who died in childbirth. Amy was trapped paying off her mother's debt to Mr. Buddy, her master. Morrison indicated that, like other women in subservient roles, Mr. Buddy's treatment of Amy was physically abusive and probably sexually abusive. As an indentured servant, Amy would have had few legal protections. Furthermore, in the isolation of the backwoods, she would have been as vulnerable as a slave. This parallel between the treatment of servants and

---

7. In addition to the issue of white indentured servants, Morrison also included representations of Native Americans. Paul D, when he escaped from the chain gang in Alfred, Georgia, ran to an Indian camp where he was welcomed. The plight of the tribe was described: "only the aged and the ill were left behind when the bulk of the tribe moved off to escape the incursions of the whites." Broken treaties, forced relocation, and the spread of European illnesses were highlighted in this section of the novel.

8. Crawley, 1999.

slaves followed a trajectory stemming from 1682, when there were no laws distinguishing a slave from a servant. However, as time moved forward and the increased importation of African slaves influenced the workforce, servant and slave codes became more entrenched in racial distinctions. Later "anti-amalgamation" and "manumission" laws became common and insured that avenues to freedom "would no longer affect the bondage of blacks or Indians,"[9] creating a racially divided system of bound labor. These codes, which will be further discussed in a subsequent chapter focusing upon indenture, distinguish Amy from Sethe based upon race and birthright. They establish Amy on the lowest rung of white supremacy.

This distinction also influences the goals of each of the runaway women: Sethe simply wants to survive whereas Amy wants to mesh into the social structures available to her. Amy knows that escape will enable her to enter into the free labor market and gain material possessions. Therefore, her flight connected to upward mobility and economic markers of liberty rather than to the physical freedom which Sethe sought. This difference was in keeping with the period of the novel's setting and reflected the various colonial slave codes which emphasized the racial distinctions that became markers of slavery. Through the character of Amy Denver, the line between servants and slaves was clearly drawn on racial lines as it was in this historical period. Sethe described the white indentured servant, Amy, as the "the raggediest-looking trash you ever saw,"[10] but due to her whiteness and her Christian ancestry, Amy held a position far superior to that of Sethe. Amy was human: only her labor— her indenture—could be bought and sold during the specified term of her contract.

The two women—servant and slave—accidentally encountered one another in the backwoods near the banks of the Mississippi River. Amy found Sethe prostrate on the ground. Having been badly beaten on the night she ran, Sethe was planning to allow herself to die when Amy arrived. Amy revived Sethe by placing spider webs across her whip wounds, leaves and moss against her swollen and inflamed feet, and massaging some of the pain away. Despite this tenderness, Amy continually disparaged Sethe's race and lack of humanity. As she helped Sethe, Amy compared her acts to the kindness she would offer to any wild beast found injured because she was "good at sick things." Amy constantly referred to Sethe as

---

9. Williams, 1994.
10. Beloved, 31.

either an animal or a thing, reemphasizing the distinctions between slave and human.

When Sethe was unable to move from the ground where she had collapsed, Amy asked her, "what you gonna do, just lay there and foal?" Nonetheless, Amy stayed with Sethe and delivered her namesake, Denver. The next morning Amy quickly disappeared because her own status would not protect her if she were caught with a runaway slave. As she had no assets, her penalty might have come in the form of a return to servitude, a risk she was certainly unwilling to take. The indenture that she had just escaped was not her own contract but instead that of her mother who had died in childbirth. Amy inherited her mother's debt and incurred additional years of service to pay for the food and lodging of her infancy. This aspect of her situation parallels some of the customs and laws of the period, but should not have been applied to her.

If a family came over via indenture or under the redemptioner system, the passage expense for any family member who died on the voyage was added to that of the remaining family members. The law stipulated that if a person died at a specified point into the passage, only half fare was required, but after that point full fare was due. The redemptioner system differed from indenture in that the traveler tended to pay a portion of his or her fare prior to expatriating and hoped to pay the balance upon arrival in the colonies. Upon arrival, the money could be acquired through trade, through the help of family members, or through a prior business arrangement. Only if the balance were left unpaid would the traveler enter into a servant contract. Oftentimes parents would contract out one of their children, while maintaining their own liberty. Again, the hopes were to become financially solvent and buy out the child's remaining contract time. Unfortunately, many of these arrangements did not work successfully and many immigrants were forced into servitude. Once contracted, the redemptioners were on equal footing with servants and one step away from slavery.

Amy's indenture seems to have been contrary to law. Amy's mother had started to fulfill her contract prior to her death and it should not have been inherited by her daughter. The explanation for this discrepancy may reflect an erroneous conception on Morrison's part or it may be further evidence that Amy's master was misusing the system because of the lack of oversight in his rural community.

Morrison's portrayal of Amy as an indentured servant came very late in the US experience, but it was historically plausible. David Galenson notes that instances of white servitude survived after the colonial period and "isolated cases of indenture in the United Sates could be found as late as the fourth decade of the nineteenth century."[11] The use of indenture in the novel enabled the racial separation between servants and slaves to be highlighted. However, in its earliest inception, indentured servitude was not tied to race. As noted earlier, the first Africans who arrived in Jamestown, Virginia by 1620 were treated as indentured servants, held to unwritten contracts. These individuals were provided with food, drink, lodging, clothing, and were given what came to be called Freedom Dues at their release. Freedom Dues varied from colony to colony, but judging from the earliest contracts held by white indentured servants, these dues typically granted the released servant with suits of clothing, shoes, and in some cases small plots of land. Amy had none of these things, which supports the assumption that she was running and places her on closer footing with Sethe.

The line differentiating the two groups, servants and slaves, was blurry until approximately 1640, when black servants in the colonies were entitled to Freedom Dues, and several of the freed servants took on servants of their own. Melvin Sylvester noted that these "Africans could become free people and enjoy some of the liberties like other new settlers."[12] Although there always existed a line between the Africans and the Europeans, the distinctions between the two groups represented by Sethe and Amy became increasingly delimitated. One of the first cases is that of John Punch, one of three servants who ran from their Virginia farm. All three men received 30 lashes upon recapture. However, the two white servants had years added to their servant contracts, whereas the third man, a black man, Punch, was condemned to a life sentence of service. By 1640, slavery became institutionalized in Maryland. In 1641, Massachusetts followed suit in its written legislative Body of Liberties.

These distinctions created an ever-widening gap between the two groups of bound labor. Nonetheless, Amy remained vulnerable for aiding Sethe. If she were a runaway herself, she would have incurred added service time, and if she were free, the power of the Fugitive Slave Act would have imperiled Amy's future. Under the developing slavery system, in contrast to the indentured servant system, the persons themselves became the property, permanently equated with livestock. In *Beloved* this point was repeatedly stressed. To reemphasize the point, when Sethe killed her daughter, she was taken into custody and tried for her crime. Her crime, however,

---

11. Galenson, 4.

12. Sylvester, Melvin. "The African American: A Journey from Slavery to Freedom."

was not murder; it was theft and destruction of property. In the text, she was tried, found guilty, and released because Schoolteacher no longer valued her as a workable asset.

Interestingly, in Morrison's operatic version of the story titled *Margaret Garner: A New American Opera*, the trial scene takes on great prominence whereas in the novel it was a side note. The Sethe character in *Beloved* is Margaret Garner in the opera. The opera emphasized the view of slaves as property and highlighted other aspects of the slave system that developed. In the novel, all four of Sethe's children were fathered by her husband, Halle, but in the opera, Margaret's children were clearly those of her master—a vivid rape scene provided evidence. Similarly, the master's pursuit of Margaret after she ran was both economically and sexually motivated. By establishing the paternity of the children in this way, the other changes in the laws governing slave status were presented. Prior to 1662, an individual's lineage and inheritance rights were traced though the paternal line; however, in the colonies, new legal provisions defined slavery as inherited through the maternal line. The operatic version may be a closer rendition of the plight of the historical account of Margaret Garner than that offered by the novel. The opera presents the legal scenario of a child born of a slave mother and free white father. According to the documents of the case, the escaped slave Margaret Garner did, in fact, kill her daughter when the slave catchers arrived; she was tried for destruction of property and remanded back to her master. According to newspaper records, one woman who attended the trial commented that Garner's ability kill her children may be explained by their paternity. She described the children as very light skinned and their master was implicated in their conception.

In any event, found guilty, Garner was remanded back to slavery but drowned when her ship met with a violent storm. In the opera, the trial scene concluded with Margaret's death sentence. While poised on the gallows, her master arrived with a last minute reprieve from the governor. While her family and her owners rejoiced at the news, Margaret, with the noose still snug against her neck, flung herself from the platform. With these three accounts, the historical Garner, the operatic Margaret, and the fictional Sethe, Morrison developed the themes of property and lineage consistent with slave law.

When considering the death scene in the opera and the novel's presentation of the thwarted existence Sethe maintained after her trial, the power of the Fugitive Slave Act makes a terrifying impact. During a short span of twenty-eight days, Sethe lived in physical freedom. She was able to care for her children and nurse her infant. Her tenuous, but joyous, claim to freedom was abruptly ruptured by the appearance of Schoolteacher. The slave catcher and sheriff were with him as well. Sethe recognized the futility of her position and knew that she and her children would be returned to the horrors of Sweet Home. Instead of allowing this, she attempted to kill her four children and herself before the slave catchers entered the shed into which she has run. Sethe drew a saw across the necks of her two boys and the older girl. She also attempted to crack the skull of her infant girl against the wall of the shed. Both the boys survived as did the baby, Denver, but the older daughter died in her mother's arms. Sethe's belief in the righteousness of her actions and her proper performance of motherhood impel the child's ghost to return to her for love and attention. The rest of the narrative moved away from the legal situation of slavery and into the complicated relationships of those who have survived the experience of the flight from Sweet Home. However, the quest for self-definition within slavery established by the characters of Halle, Sixo, Paul D, and Sethe in the beginning of the novel created a fundamental concept which was touched upon in Morrison's other fiction: the impact of slavery reached far beyond the experiences of the slaves themselves. And, although its legacy created various avenues for growth, it was the historical events of slavery and its aftermath that framed much of Morrison's characters' development.

This backdrop can be seen quite clearly in Morrison's novel *Song of Solomon*. The Emancipation Proclamation and its broken promises of undisturbed freedom permeated the tales in *Song of Solomon*. Abraham Lincoln 1863 statement reads as follows:

> All persons held as slaves within any State or designated part of a State, the people whereof shall then be in rebellion against the United States, shall be then, thenceforward, and forever free; and the Executive Government of the United States, including the military and naval authority thereof, will recognize and maintain the freedom of such persons, and *will do no act or acts to repress such persons, or any of them, in any efforts they may make for their actual freedom* [italics mine].[13]

Unfortunately, the historical events following the emancipation of the slaves belied the paternalistic tenor of Lincoln's pronouncement. The Reconstruction period, which lasted from 1866 to 1877, was a time of great upheaval for the country and few felt the ramifications of this turmoil as

---

13. Lincoln, 1863.

painfully as the freed slaves.[14] *Song of Solomon* encompassed this period through the character of Macon Dead. Having been granted his freedom, Macon focused upon land acquisition and economic independence.[15] Like the character of Amy Denver, and different from the slaves in *Beloved*, his newly decided legal status granted him the physical liberty dreamed of by captive slaves. With Singing Bird,[16] his Native American wife, Macon Dead (Jake)[17] traveled north to completely disconnect from his slave past. His goal was simple: buy land and develop a farm that would provide for his growing family. Macon met with success despite a series of discriminatory acts perpetrated against him by the whites he encountered.

Although the protection promised by the Emancipation Proclamation quickly proved to be empty rhetoric, Macon's plans came to fruition. He was able to acquire land and turn it into a working farm; however, its beauty and profitability inspired jealousy in the locals. Unwittingly, Macon signed a paper allowing these men to claim his land which was poignantly named Lincoln's Heaven. The legal document laying claim to Lincoln's Heaven as well as the socially sanctioned actions against Macon, enforced by police, replicated experiences of ex-slaves in the period. The day the men came to take possession of the farm, Macon resisted them: reprisal for this refusal was that they "shoot him five feet in the air." Despite the fact that Macon's land and life were taken from him, he became a model for his children. Much like the character of Sixo, Macon's self-definition existed outside of the parameters set by others. Through the character of

---

14. "Blacks were subjected to both official punishment by local authorities and unofficial sanctioning at the hands of vigilante mobs. This was a lethal combination, resulting in the legal execution of nearly 3,000 blacks between 1880 and 1935 and the extra-legal lynching of an additional 3,000 blacks during the same period" (Tolnay, Beck, and Massey, 1992).

15. Part of the issue faced by Macon Dead and his desire to acquire land stem from the "refusal of Congress to redistribute land to ex-*slaves* and poor whites, thereby depriving ex-*slaves* an economic base for independence and inhibiting a coalition between blacks and poor whites that would have operated against a native white political backlash" (Hunston, 2005).

16. Morrison used the character of Singing Bird to include the plight of Native Americans in the representation of American history. However, Morrison also made clear the distinction between the treatments the two groups received: Singing Bird "always bragged how she was never a slave. Her people neither" (Beloved).

17. Singing Bird, whose family disapproved of her love for an ex-slave, took off with Jake (Macon Dead I) at the end of the war to create a life away from parental disapproval. In fact, it was Singing Bird who convinced Jake to keep the name Macon Dead to avoid her family's discovery.

Macon and his son, Morrison emphasized the fragility of life as a freed slave and created a scenario which traced the legacy of slavery. In particular, Macon's son must come to terms with the life he had inherited. The action of the novel moved rapidly forward and included two significant time periods: the Jim Crow south as well as the advent of the Civil Rights Movement.

The son, a second Macon Dead, who will be referred to as Dead, used the law to ensure personal freedom based upon economic prosperity. Having watched his father's labors and murder, Dead fixated upon upward mobility and land acquisition as the markers of freedom. He strove to meet and beat the white man at his own game. When Macon was killed by the locals, there was no way for his two young children to find justice. Since there was a signed document, the legal system supported the locals' right to the land. Both Dead and his sister Pilate are told they were in jeopardy for having witnessed the murder. The children, knowing that they were unprotected by the law, ran from their land and their home. With this background, Dead's preoccupation with the legal acquisition of wealth was an understandable development even if it becomes unsavory. Dead's blind ambition became the attainment of success in "the white man world" while matching and surpassing his father's success. Sadly, instead of freedom, Dead became trapped by the very assets he believed would liberate him.

Dead's middle class strivings transpired during The Jim Crow era. This was the period of the Separate but Equal doctrine, which dated to the 1896 *Plessy v. Ferguson* decision.[18] The backdrop to this case was the event of June 7, 1892 in which Homer Plessy, one-eighths black and seven-eighths white, was jailed for sitting in the "White" car of the East Louisiana Railroad. In *Homer Adolph Plessy v. The State of Louisiana*, Plessy argued that the Separate Car Act violated the Thirteenth and Fourteenth Amendments to the Constitution.[19] The judge at the trial was John Howard Ferguson, a lawyer from Massachusetts who had previously declared the Separate Car Act 'unconstitutional on trains that traveled through several states.'[20] In Plessy's case, however, Ferguson decided that the state could choose to regulate railroad companies that operated within Louisiana. Plessy was found guilty of refusing to leave the white car. In an appeal to Supreme Court

---

18. For more on the Plessy decision see Richard Kluger's *Simple Justice: The History of Brown v. Board of Education and Black America's Struggle for Equality.*

19. Louisiana History, 1.

20. Cozzens, 1.

of Louisiana, Ferguson's decision was upheld. In a subsequent case, in 1896, the Supreme Court of the United States once again found Plessy guilty. This court case set the foundation for the entire Separate but Equal policy that allowed the legal separation of whites and blacks in all areas of public activity.

Song of Solomon utilized and emphasized this policy in several instances: Dead's wife, Ruth Foster, was the "first colored expectant mother ... allowed to give birth inside [the white hospital's] wards and not on its steps." Yet, this was the same hospital where Ruth's father, Dr. Foster, was banned from practicing because of his race. Despite these affronts, Dead's desire to own a lakefront home in the wealthy black community of Honére was heightened by its proximity to the property of whites. His desire for economic equality, and ultimately social acceptance, was embodied by this property. Similarly, his desire to break the barrier created by Jim Crow was also reflected in the car he drove. He bought the biggest car possible, yet drove it far too slowly, and only used it to take his family on miserable treks to the resort town. Where Dead believed this acquisition marked him as a member of the rising middle class, the attitude of the townspeople toward Dead and his car emphasized their divergent imaginations of the good life:

> Macon's wide green Packard belied what they thought a car was for. He never went over twenty miles an hour, never gunned his engine, never stayed in first gear for a block or two to give pedestrians a thrill ... so they called it Macon Dead's Hearse.[21]

Dead was firmly entrenched in his desire to ingratiate himself into the high opinion of white businessmen so much so that he could not recognize the derision of the townsfolk for what it was: he believed their scorn was simply generated by jealousy instead of a more nuanced disapproval.

Nonetheless, despite their contempt, Dead was "feared as a tyrant by his community and his own family. Instead of conceptualizing injustice as the racism his community confronts daily, Macon personalizes injustice."[22] The character of Dead embodied the corrupting power of the Jim Crow regulations: he had ingested the racist model. He not only relished his economic power and privilege, but also replicated the oppressive system of racial and class distinctions. He utilized property and the law much in the same vein as the locals who had stolen his childhood home. He envisioned

---

21. Song of Solomon, 32.
22. Storhoff, 293.

himself to be separate from the other blacks in town and equal to the propertied whites, the fallacy of which he only slowly became aware.

As he strove to possess land, accumulating apartment after apartment in the black section of town, and collecting rent and debt with ferocity, he began to inhabit a middle zone of existence. Never to be accepted into white culture, legally or socially, his desire for wealth borders upon megalomania. So powerful is his desire to retaliate against the oppressive white power structure, that he unwittingly allows himself to become its servant. Because Dead's fight for social integration and legal equality was an individual effort, which used the blacks around him as cannon fodder, he was seen as an enemy and a traitor. Dead was perceived as being not only just as bad as the white people but worse. He paralleled the figure of a plantation overseer in the Antebellum South, who—through connection to the power structure—became a more ridged and brutal taskmaster than the original model. With this comparison, the novel touched directly upon the way in which the psychology of slavery corrupted slaves. Eugene Genovese explained how some slaves "tried to raise their own image in society at the expense of other slaves," and noted that "simultaneously they were narrowing the distance between white and black. They felt superior to the poor whites and even to some solid yeomen."[23] Dead took his cue from this legacy of slavery. He felt superior to the poor whites and saw himself on equal footing with all but the wealthiest. Unfortunately, in order to maintain his superiority, Dead had to sever ties with most of the members of the black community and replicate the system of legal and economic abuse against them.

Most significantly, Dead's associations with white businessmen kept him estranged from his sister, Pilate. His goals could only be attained through upward mobility which forced him to override his yearning to reconnect to her. Pilate's response to the loss of land and her father's death was diametrically opposed to that of her brother. Where he sought wealth and respectability, she eschewed possession and shunned social convention. Her lifestyle was entirely casual, but by no means uncaring. She focused her energies on her daughter and granddaughter, earning money sometimes as a bootlegger and sometimes as a trader, but accumulating just enough to get by. Therefore, while Dead focused upon middle class values, Pilate fully embraced her life in the lowest echelon of society. As a result, Dead was afraid of her influence upon his hard earned re-

---

23. Genovese, 328.

spectability and perceived her lifestyle as a direct threat to his future. He demanded that Pilate explain "What [she is] trying to make [him] look like in this town?" Significantly, when he says town, he means the white businessmen. Because of the dual power systems in the Jim Crow era, Dead's devotion to the white economic power structure increased his vulnerability:

> He trembled with the thought of the white men in the bank—
> the men who helped him buy and mortgage houses—discover-
> ing that this raggedy bootlegger was his sister. That the propertied
> Negro who handled his business so well and who lived in the big
> house on Not Doctor Street had a sister who had a daughter but
> no husband, and that daughter had a daughter but no husband.
> A collection of lunatics who made wine and sang in the streets
> "like common street women! Just like common street women!"[24]

Much more than adhering to the codes of the middle class, Macon was caught up in his own fantasy of what white middle class values were. This middle class ideal kept him lurking outside of Pilate's window when he crept up to listen to his sister and her family singing the songs of his youth. Although he "felt himself softening under the weight of memory and music,"[25] he did not enter. Rather than entering, Dead was bound to the precepts of respectability. He could not relinquish his elitist attitudes because that would jeopardize his definition of success. If he were to recognize beauty in his sister, to acknowledge that her chaotic, scrambling way of life was on a par with his middle class existence, his fantasy would rupture. Such a rupture would call into question all of his life choices, most primarily his choice of Ruth Foster as his wife.

Dead selected Ruth not for herself but because her father was "the most important Negro in the city."[26] Her money and her light skin fitted neatly into his plan. Blinded by his desire to marry the child of the prestigious Dr. Foster, Dead did not sense Ruth's oddities. Similarly, Dead placed so much value on his own economic power that he was convinced this was the reason that Dr. Foster granted him Ruth's hand in marriage. He did not realize that the doctor had "begun to chafe under her devotion," and that Ruth's "steady beam of love" directed at him had become "unsettling." Instead, Dead overlooked his misgivings. Much later, when he found Ruth

---

24. Song of Solomon, 20.
25. Song of Solomon, 30.
26. Song of Solomon, 96.

with her father's corpse "lying next to him. Naked as a yard dog, kissing him. Him dead and white and puffy and skinny, and she had his fingers in her mouth,"[27] his desire to maintain respectability enabled him to override the implications of his wife's behavior. Dead ignored this event just as he tolerated the underlying insecurities of his children's parentage. His desire to protect his claim on the middle class superseded his revulsion towards his wife, his hatred of his father-in-law, his contempt for his children, and his longing for his sister. His desire to cross the legal lines established by Jim Crow outweighed all other concerns.

In *Song of Solomon,* Morrison traced the legacy of slavery and the repercussions of legal structures into a third generation. The third Macon Dead, whose nickname was Milkman, occupies the period in which the Jim Crow laws were beginning to shift and social structures were ever more fluid. In contrast to his father Dead, Milkman rejected the ideal of economic superiority and the promise of class advancement. Milkman and his best friend, Guitar Bains, lived at the cusp of the Civil Rights movement and had been influenced by freedoms disallowed by the restrictive periods experienced by Macon and Dead. The Separate but Equal policy under which Dead developed his obsessions had come to a close. The *Brown v Board of Education* trial of 1954 had put an end to segregation.[28] Therefore, Milkman occupied a liminal space in history between the legacies of slavery—Reconstruction and Jim Crow—and complete integration won by the Civil Rights Movement. This precarious position was traced through Milkman's relationships to his family and to the townspeople with whom he associated: both were conflicted. He struggled against the racist and discriminatory attitudes of his home environment, which was steeped in class consciousness. Yet, his conception of the value of the legal gains made was vague and untethered.

In his youth, Milkman developed in simple opposition to his father. He rejected Dead's desires for him to become a businessman, working for him only to secure pocket money and the excuse to loiter in the rough area of town where Dead owned property. Milkman's struggle to be rid of the middle-class restrictions and expectations held by both his parents was

---

27. Song of Solomon, 73.

28. The Supreme Court's Oliver Brown v. Board of Education of Topeka decision did not abolish segregation in public areas, such as restaurants, buses, and restrooms, nor did it require desegregation of public schools by a specific time. It did, however, declare the permissive or mandatory segregation that existed in 21 states unconstitutional.

part of an adolescent search for identity. Subsequently, his development incorporates a conscious rejection of white standards and white power structures. The contempt Milkman felt for his father's line of work, and the economic and legal blackmail Dead employed, became anchored in his desire to refute the business practices of whites. Milkman aligned himself with the black community, which saw Dead as a sell-out, and discovered the world occupied by his aunt Pilate.

On a journey which Milkman takes ostensibly to search for his grandfather's buried gold, he fulfilled the requirements outlined in a as he traveled into the Deep South. As he moves farther and farther south, the trappings of his world were removed from him and he was confronted with value systems outside the opposing poles represented by his materialistic father and his reactionary friend Guitar. Eventually he met men who remembered his grandfather and a woman who helped raise his father. The stories Milkman heard about each Macon Dead filled him with pride. Beyond his development of an independent self, capable of action and taking responsibility for the outcome of those actions, Milkman encountered situations which enabled him to perceive the legal structures that had formed both his father and grandfather. His newfound understanding informed his response to his friend Guitar and their mutual plan to retaliate against white oppression.

Prior to the development of this insight, Milkman had been mired in a revenge plot orchestrated by Guitar and a vigilante group, The Seven Days. The group's response to the consequences of slavery, the structures of Jim Crow, and the backlash against the Civil Rights Movement was to institute a series of violent reprisals. In this way, Guitar functioned as a foil to Dead. Where Dead wanted to earn money and gain acceptance into white society, Guitar wanted to steal Macon's gold to fund the destruction of white schoolgirls.[29] This particular desire was fueled by The Seven Days, which returned violence against blacks with violence against whites.

For Guitar, however, the violent reaction to the bombing of The Sixteenth Street Baptist Church in Birmingham and the murder of Emmitt Till[30] did

---

29. Here Morrison evoked the Birmingham Church bombing in which four school girls were killed as they attended Sunday School. Although the time line is off, the event took place almost 10 years after the murder of Emmitt Till, the town of Birmingham suffered over 50 bombings of black institutions between the years 1947 and 1965.

30. On Aug. 27, 1955, Emmett Till, aged 14, allegedly whistled at a white woman. Her husband Roy Bryant and his half-brother, J.W. Milam, yanked Till out of his bed in the middle of the night. They then proceeded to beat the boy, after which they shot him to death and disposed of his body in the Tallahatchie River in Mississippi. At the

not remain targeted against whites. Guitar's rage eventually mutated and he not only accidentally killed Pilate but also actively hunted down Milkman in the southern woods. The conclusion of the novel presented a condemnation of the laws of slavery and its legacies as well as a warning against complete refutation of the rule of law.

In *Song of Solomon*, Morrison developed her characters as they moved through the legal structures which follow the trajectory of slavery through Reconstruction, Jim Crow, to land in the midst of the Civil Rights Movement. By utilizing historical events, the characters were neatly contextualized and the motivations for their behavior take on resonance outside of the narrative. Just as Dead's class strivings could be understood under the rubric of the Separate but Equal doctrine, Guitar's bloodlust developed a certain logic within the violent lead up to the passage of The Civil Rights Act of 1964. The echoes of slavery and the ramifications of racially contentious history found in this text link back to and expand upon Morrison's development of legal issues in *Beloved*.

---

trial, both men were exonerated of the crime after 67 minutes of deliberation. January 1956, Roy Bryant openly acknowledged the murder in an interview for *Look Magazine*.

Chapter Four

The Laws of Indentured Servitude: Fact and Fiction in Literature[1]

The laws of indenture were relatively straight forward. Although there were several different ways in which the indenture system was subdivided, the common legal arrangement was the voluntary contract between servant and master. The average contract ran between 5–7 years, and it was usually entered into as a means for an individual to secure transport from Europe to the British colonies. This seemingly benign method of contract employment, which often functioned according to plan, was nonetheless often compromised through the rupture of its legal structures. Literary representations of the system's abuse came in the form of contemporary first person narratives, personal correspondence, and modern day fictional accounts. Two narratives presented here describe situations of women who were tricked into service, illegally bound or whose contract was illegally extended. One contemporary autobiographical account, that of William Moraley in his work titled *The Infortunate*, offered a different and sometimes problematic account of his indentured servant's experience. When compared to other writings by indentured servants, as well as the accounts generated through historically based creation, Moraley seemed to have been most fortunate in his circumstances. Yet, despite his relatively positive experience, his narrative described exploitation of servants and it reported upon the legal manipulations which increased contractual obligations of indentured servants. These legal manipulations were commented upon in all the subsequent narratives presented.

Beginning with Kate McCafferty's 2002 work *Testimony of an Irish Slave Girl*, which detailed the plight of the fictional Cot Daley, the first instance

---

1. A portion of this chapter appeared in the 2006 Texas Wesleyan Law Review under the title of "Codifying Humanity: The Legal Line between Slave and Servant" and an earlier version was presented at the " 'Too Pure an Air:' Law and the Quest for Freedom, Justice, and Equality" conference held at the University of Gloucester, England. 18 Jun 2006.

of malfeasance was presented: kidnapping into service. Through her narrative, Cot detailed her young life first in Ireland then as an indentured servant in Barbados. Although not ideal, her childhood in Ireland was that of a respectable under-classed family. Unfortunately, one winter's day, while caroling with other children from her village, Cot was swept up in one of the nets of Oliver Cromwell's men, who were sent to Ireland to cleanse the country of the natives refusing to relinquish their land.[2] This policy created an Irish slave trade where captives were transported to Barbados (from which the term Barbadosed came) and sold as indentured servants. The sweeps of Ireland extended beyond the deportation of political dissidents and moved into random, opportunistic capture of unprotected men, women, and children. Cot was one of these children who were sold to British planters in the islands. The number of Irish who were Barbadosed is unknown and estimates vary widely,[3] as high as 60,000 to a lower estimate of 12,000,[4] yet it was known that the Irish intermingled with African slaves and joined in the slave revolts on the island. The story that Cot shared was called a testimony to reflect her indictment as a member of a mixed-race plot to overthrow the slaveholding system. And her tale told of the worst possible treatment suffered as an indentured servant.

As an abducted child, Cot was bereft of all familial or social support and she had no legal recourse whatsoever. Her predicament was generated by a twofold problem. The first aspect related to her captivity itself. The fact that she was stolen, spirited away, rather than legally indentured was something that she could not prove. Her claim to freedom was either unheard or disregarded. She held no papers to prove her free status because as a free citizen in Ireland there was no need for such documentation. In keeping with this lack of evidence, Cot's captivity was compounded by the fact that she was a young girl from the lower class. Her father would

---

2. James F. Cavanaugh, in Irish Slavery states that "On 14 August 1652, Cromwell began his Ethnic Cleansing of Ireland, ordering that the Irish were to be transported overseas, starting with 12,000 Irish prisoners sold to Barbados. The infamous 'Connaught or Hell' proclamation was issued on 1 May 1654, where all Irish were ordered to be removed from their lands and relocated west of the Shannon or be transported to the West Indies."

3. In England's Irish Slaves, Robert E. West cites that "1652, prior to the wholesale transportation of Irish, most of 12 thousand political prisoners on Barbados were Irish."

4. http://www.yale.edu/glc/tangledroots/Barbadosed.htm.

have had limited resources, both economic and political, to devote to Cot's rescue. Similarly, Cot's youth, class, and gender would have made her an uninteresting focus for local magistrates. The power of Cromwell, and the soldiers who acted in his name, made Cot's plight dismissible for magistrates interested in her return. In order to fight on her behalf, any lawyer would have requested appropriate compensation for the inherent risk in pursuing the issue. Moving against the British was dangerous and only significant incentive would have propelled a member of the legal community to act against the crown, and Cot's father did not have enough coin to create such an incentive.

Therefore, once Cot was captured, she was utterly lost to both her father and her homeland. She became fully ensconced in the role of an indentured servant, removed from the limited legal protections provided by Irish citizenship. This fictional account reflected historical information such as that cited by Robert E. West, who noted the British agenda to send Irish Catholic children to "into slavery in the West Indies, Virginia and New England, [so] that they might lose their faith and all knowledge of their nationality" and the 20,000 to 30,000 Irish adults who were sold into slavery irrespective of their previous social station.[5] In the midst of this tumultuous period, a young child such as Cot would have vanished without comment by the larger community that had been decimated by the actions of Cromwell's troops.

Once entangled in the servant system, the second aspect of Cot's experience in captivity became apparent. Unlike Moraley, who operated very much as a free agent throughout his indenture, Cot was confronted by multiple situations and individuals who represented the cruelest types of masters. These individuals were concerned with the profit that could be made from servants' labor rather than any type of even exchange proffered by the indentured servant contract. McCafferty in her portrayal of Cot's life, took great pain to explicate the variety of ways in which an indentured servant could be used and misused.

One of the more salient points McCafferty made through the narrative was the liquid nature of contracts, unlike their implied codification. According to the laws governing indentured, there were legitimate ways in which a contract could be extended. These conditions most often focused upon

---

5. E. Williams reports: "In 1656 Cromwell's Council of State voted that 1,000 Irish girls and 1,000 Irish young men be sent to Jamaica." (15)

events when a servant had ruptured the agreement for which the contract owner was allowed to demand recompense. Typical events that would garner extended work time were generated by a servant's inability to work: extended periods of illness or, for women, pregnancy[6] could add years of compensation to a worker's time. Another issue that became increasingly more common was the extension of contracts as punishment for running away or hindering production in other ways. If a servant ran, the courts would consider various factors when assigning service to the recaptured runaway to reimburse for the master's lost earnings. These costs would be adjudicated by the local courts which decided upon compensation. Factors beyond the labor lost would also be factored into the time extension of a servant's contract. These included costs associated with tracking and apprehending the runaway, jail costs, and any other legal fees connected with the case. These justifiable extensions were often misapplied to servants innocent of bad acts, or bad faith, and this was the situation confronted by Cot as she moved through several mercenary owners of her contract.

The terms of her servitude were repeatedly expanded, her contract being either sold and rewritten or unjustly extended through false accusations of bad behavior. When McCafferty's novel opens, the adult Cot was reflecting back upon 29 years in service and the events which brought her into the legal system and forced her confession. Tended to by the jail's apothecary, Dr. Peter Coote, Cot weaves a chaotic tale reflecting the vagaries of her life. In her testimony, a rambling affair broken by bouts of fever and collapse, Cot cited the Proclamation of 1657.[7] This Proclamation, in her words, described the Irish as "slothful and dissolute, lewd, evil, and pilfering," and granted the ability for any Constable to whip any Irish servant they suspected of counterfeiting a master's permission ticket to walk on the streets. She noted that any runaways should be flogged and that their "service lengthen between two years and double."[8] It was due to this

---

6. In Differential Tolerances and Accepted Punishments for Disobedient Indentured Servants and Their Masters in Colonial Court, Melissa A. Roe cites the evidence of contract extension for pregnant servants: "While servants in Prince Georges County were obviously sentenced to fewer extra days (188 days) than their counterparts in York County (398 days), servants in Prince Georges County were whipped as both a punishment and deterrent to other servants."

7. Cromwell, Oliver. A Proclamation by His Highness and the Parliament. London: Printed by Henry Hills and John Field, 1657.

8. McCafferty, 90.

proclamation[9] that Cot's contract was first unfairly expanded beyond its original terms. The second extension came in response to her drunken rage in which she attempted to beat an overseer who had broken up an Easter Sunday party. Citing the *Act for the Ordaining of Rights between Masters and Servants,*[10] Cot explained that she was lashed and that two more years were added to her service. Although punishment for her attempted violence was warranted by the system, the voluminous extension of service time was not. The addition of two years increased her service debt by over one-third.

Each episode in Cot's rendition focused upon the corruption of the system which irrevocably bound her. Her standard seven-year contract had been incrementally extended twenty-two years beyond its initial parameters, and all these added years were based either upon exaggerated reactions to her behavior or false charges. Only the closing acts of her life, her participation in a slave rebellion, merited the punishments exacted earlier. In fact, in one early incident, she had reported an insurrection plot to her master but received punishment along with the conspirators. After a grueling life of drudgery, abuse, and personal loss, Cot gave up the hope that she would ever be freed and became a committed drinker and a genuine rebel.

Toward the end of her life, having lost children from previous unions through death or removal, Cot had been placed in a union with an African slave for the clear purpose of producing children. Although unhappy with her situation and horrified at becoming a third wife to a non-white, non-christian, Cot eventually became invested in her non-traditional family. Through the birth of her children, Cot became emotionally linked to her husband, and she was eventually accepted by the extended family and ultimately trusted them. Through her union, Cot became aware of a brewing slave revolt and enlisted herself as both messenger and arms carrier. *Testimony of an Irish Slave Girl* accurately portrayed the historical rebellion of 1675, the second major slave rebellion in Barbados. The plot had been brewing for three years and was only uncovered through one slave's betrayal.[11] Cot's role in this revolt paralleled the unity between the servant

---

9. Laws of Barbados. http://www.archive.org/stream/cu31924017514427/cu3192401 7514427_djvu.txt.

10. W. Noel Sainsbury (editor). "America and West Indies: December 1661." Calendar of State Papers Colonial, America and West Indies, Volume 5: 1661–1668 (1880): 61–66.

11. The island-wide rebellion seems to have been three years in the planning when it was uncovered through the betrayal of a slave woman named Fortuna: "colonial of-

and slave groups. And like the slaves and servants found guilty of insurrection, her sentence was death. At no point in her testimony did Cot attempt to hide her participation in the plot or to circumvent her punishment. Although her confessional was coerced through the ministrations of the apothecary, it became abundantly clear that Cot had turned the situation, if not her advantage, to her own purpose.

Her audience, the prejudging condescending Dr. Coote, had given her an avenue to describe the destruction of her life. Cot knew her testimony would be read only for the information regarding the plot and so she took the opportunity to describe and explore the reasons for the rebellion. Using both details of the slaves' lives and the ways in which her own life had unraveled under the indentured servant system, Cot condemned the legal structures that allowed such abuses. Her conclusions painted masters in unredemptive terms which precluded all possibility that the system could ever foster an equitable exchange. The corruption of law presented in this novel differed from the second fictional account of indenture presented here, *Bound*; yet, both novels shared a common theme of abuse of contract laborers as well as detailed portrayals of the plight of indentured servants and the particularly vulnerable position of women.

Bound, the second fictional account, was written by Sally Gunning in 2008. Less literary than McCafferty's work, the novel developed the legal conditions faced by a young woman indentured in New England. The novel balanced its representations of both benevolent and malevolent servitude. In the first instance, the main character Alice Cole was treated much like a child of her first owner. She was inculcated into her master's family, educated alongside the family's only daughter, Nabby, who became her closest friend and confidant, and lived in an environment about which Cot Daily Quashey[12] could only have dreamed. Part of the reason that Alice first received an equitable situation was tied to the circumstances of her indenture. Unlike Cot, who was spirited away, Alice arrived to New England under the redemptioner program outlined earlier and explored in greater detail later in the discussion of William Moraley. This system should have guaranteed that only her parents would work off the passage, or if

---

ficials arrested more than 100 alleged conspirators and tortured them until they named others. The court found nearly 50 slaves guilty of rebellion and sentenced them to be executed. At least 6 were burned alive; 11 more were beheaded and their bodies dragged through the streets of Speightstown. Five slaves committed suicide before they could be executed."

12. Quashey was Cot's married name.

that was unrealistic, that the children would labor and live with their family. It was clear from the opening of the narrative that Alice's parents had planned to quickly establish themselves as free agents upon their arrival in the colonies.

They had traveled from London to Philadelphia with plans for a new and exciting life. However, the voyage over was treacherous. First Alice's mother and then her two older brothers die of illness during transit. The gruesome travel conditions, bad storms, low rations, and high death rates accurately presented the situation faced by many crossing the Atlantic. However, the loss of three family members was an extreme representation. The death toll of this voyage, when compared to the one member lost on the *Mayflower*, may have exaggerated the situation. Still, death and disease were constant companions of transatlantic travel. Gunning's presentation of the facts of why Alice was separated from her father upon arriving in Philadelphia was also unclear. Therefore, one must surmise that the two situations were plot devices constructed to connect several aspects of indentured experiences. In particular, the harsh stipulations of some contracts were highlighted by demonstrating how the previous arrangement made by the Cole family had been dissolved with the loss of three members of the family. Alice and her father were placed in the dire position of paying off the passage of five people, three of whom were dead. Alice overheard part of her father's negotiations in which one man said, "Dead after half the voyage still means full fare."[13] And with that, Alice was sized up by the trader and sold into an indenture by her father, never to be seen again.

The contract, written in 1756, bound Alice to an eleven year stint as a servant. This was an usually long period[14] which was attributable to her youth and the fact that as a seven-year old she would require training and support until she became a productive servant. In any case, the legal issues which were focused upon in this narrative had much less to do with the appropriateness of contract terms and much more to do with lack of rights for indentured servants, particularly women. Specifically, the novel traced the change in Alice's masters to highlight the vulnerability of female servants and the potential for their sexual abuse. Upon the marriage of her

---

13. This stipulation was part of the redemptioner system in which one family member was liable for the fare of another who died in transit to the colonies.

14. In some locations, such as Maryland, it was not uncommon for children to be indentured until the age of maturity. If this applied to Alice's Philadelphia contract, then it would be reasonable for a seven-year-old child to be held to a contract of eleven years, the age of maturity being eighteen.

mistress/friend Nabby, Alice's contract was assumed by the groom, Emery Verley.

Colonial law discriminated against women, and Alice's fate was twice complicated by this fact. Because the colonies used the Common Law view of married women as *feme covert*, Nabby's legal rights and her property were merged with her husband's. Alice's contract became Verely's possession.[15] Later on in the novel, Alice's position as an unmarried woman without a husband's protection would prove even more problematic. However, at this point in the narrative, Alice had just reached physical maturity and was described as beautiful. Her beauty may have been the temptation that attracted her new owner's unwanted sexual aggression, but what Gunning made clear was that Alice's proximity and her dependency were the real enticements. Verely wanted her, in part, as a demonstration of his power over Alice and his wife. The period Alice lived with Nabby and Verley, as well as after she escaped to take up residence with a widow named Lyddie Berry, portrayed the aggression and abuse suffered by servants and their inability to defend themselves or receive legal redress.

Alice's plight had heightened restrictions because of her position as a woman under the legal codes of the eighteenth century. Compounding this legal structure were the narrative threads which placed Alice in the role of seductress, thief, and murderer. All of these accusations were false, but with her limited legal status and lack of corroboration to support her claims, Alice became a focus of the court and faced two unsavory outcomes in two separate trials: in the first instance, the threat was the return to her abusive owner and in the second case, the outcome could enact the death penalty.

In the first trial, Alice's counsel,[16] Eben Freeman, needed to invalidate Alice's contract despite her debt of three years' service. With Alice being unable to speak on her own behalf, Freeman was her only formal ally. Luckily, the Widow Berry, Freeman's lover, convinced him to represent Alice in both cases. When the first case failed to break Alice's contract, it was Berry who purchased the remainder of the indenture to

---

15. In some instances, women were protected from the full force of coverture through pre-marital agreements. These agreements safeguarded a woman's inherited property and protected her dower, a one-third lifetime interest in the real estate.

16. Under colonial law, criminal defendants had the right to legal representation. These rights were stipulated by The Massachusetts Body of Liberties, Connecticut's Fundamental Laws, the Concessions of the West Jersey Proprietors, in 1677, and the Frame of Government of Pennsylvania. (Hall, 372).

prevent Alice's return to Verley. In the second case, the murder trial, Alice was once again prohibited from directly presenting the events of her infant's death. She was required to relay her story through the voice of Freeman.

Although this made a smooth narrative tale, it was less convincing in the court room. Freeman needed to first convince the court that Alice was not guilty of fornication, a punishable offence,[17] because she had been raped, and then he had to explain that her newborn died naturally rather than being suffocated by Alice. Oddly, innocence of one act seemed to imply guilt for the other. The logic ran that if Alice's child had been a product of rape by her master, the runaway would have been more capable of infanticide.[18] Luckily, her advocate had solid standing as a defender of liberty. His reputation, only slightly marred by his fraternization with Widow Berry, as a nascent freedom fighter against the soon to be British enemy gave him sway in the community. Therefore, Alice was released although she was not completely exonerated of her crimes in the public sphere.

This representation of women under the laws governing the contracts of indentured servants, despite its somewhat happy ending, stresses the vulnerability of those held in service. Similar to the situation of Cot Quashey described by McCafferty in *Testimony*, in *Bound* Gunning developed the particularly defenseless conditions of indentured women and the facility with which they became sexual targets. In contrast, William Moraley's narrative described the position of a male servant who had volunteered for service, but who nonetheless witnessed problematic circumstances created by the indentured servant and slave systems.

---

17. For colonial lawgivers and judges "there was no clear line of demarcation between crime and sin. The pious person was law-abiding; the dissolute of spirit would or had committed crimes. This association was natural in a society that prosecuted Protestant religious dissent and threatened Roman Catholics with death. What is more, sinful activities such as drunkenness, failure to attend church, and fornication made up the vast majority of criminal prosecutions in both the mother country and her North American colonies." The application of this logic can be seen in both of the misdemeanors cases of the female indentured servants presented here: Cot Quashey was punished for drunkenness and Alice Cole for fornication. See Hall, Kermit L. ed. The Oxford Companion to American Law. Oxford UP, Oxford. 2002.

18. This argument runs parallel to the discussion of Margate Garner's trial. In like vein, one witness believed that her act of infanticide may have been less egregious than similar acts because Garner had been repeatedly impregnated by her master.

In *The Infortunate: The Voyage And Adventures Of William Moraley, An Indentured Servant,*[19] an autobiography first published in 1743,[20] the narrator set up the stark contrast between the condition of servants and slaves in the British colonies of North America. Moraley had contracted out his own labor as an indentured servant, unlike the earlier two narratives in which one servant was stolen and falsely tied to a contract and the other whose parent had signed the indenture on her behalf. Moraley held a comparatively elevated position as both an adult male and an individual who was trained and educated in higher levels of English society. From his vantage point, he noted the discrepancies in treatment of individual within bound service.

In particular, he noted the dramatic contrast between the indentured servants and the slaves in America. This contrast was distinct from the conditions in Barbados described in *Testimony*, and even Moraley, a somewhat jaded and self-serving individual, was struck by the disparity. He stated that "the Condition of the Negroes is very bad, by reason of the Severity of the Laws, there being no Laws made in Favor of these unhap[p]y Wretches" [original spelling retained].[21] And, although Moraley himself later proved to be quite an unreliable narrator,[22] he nonetheless offered

---

19. The original title was *The Infortunate: or, the Voyage and Adventures of William Moraley, of Moraley, in the country of Nothumberland, Gent-{leman,} — From his Birth, to the Present Time. Containing Whatever is Curious and Remarkable in the Provinces of Pen-{n}-sylvania and New Jersey: an Account of the Laws and Customs of the Inhabitants; the Product, Soil and Climate; also the Author's Several Adventures though Divers Parts of America, and His surprising Return to Newcastle. To which is Added His Case, Recommended to the Gentlemne of the Law* (Infortunate xix). Moraley, W., Smith, B.G. & Klepp, S.E., *The Infortunate: The Voyage And Adventures Of William Moraley, An Indentured Servant.* Pennsylvania State U P, University Park. 1992.

20. This autobiography has been rediscovered, edited, and reprinted by Susan E Klepp and Billy Gordon Smith. The 1992 edition has been annotated with supplemental information, historical documents, and images. Additionally the editors have provided introductory information which fleshes out the political, economic, and religious conditions of England during the 1700s, the situations of indentured servants in America, and the particular circumstances related to William Moraley's condition. The appendices provide genealogical information as well as maps and a description of Moraley's life after the close of his autobiography.

21. Moraley, 53.

22. Problems with Moraley's representations range from inaccurate details of fauna and flora, miscalculations of population and other statistics, as well as ellipses in his narrative. It is clear from the onset of the narrative that Moraley intends to sell his tale for profit: this may in part explain the diverse subjects mention in the subtitle to his autobiography. Each item may appeal to various buyers as he strives to incorporate as much adventure and information as possible in his account.

valuable perspective on the various types of servants and slaves found in 18th century colonial America.

At the time Moraley penned his autobiography, the system distinguishing servant from slave was becoming increasingly rigid.[23] Various colonial laws[24] had begun the process of codifying African servants, who came to the shores involuntarily, as separate and distinct from the servants who entered into contractual agreements. However, in the earliest instance, 1620, the individuals brought from Africa to colonial American shores functioned as indentured servants.[25] There were no records marking the auctioning of these individuals or providing their terms of service, yet there was evidence which demonstrated that after time elapsed, these Africans were allowed to enter into society as free people. Later documents verified that the earliest African brought to British colonial shores not only obtained their freedom after a period of servitude, but some went on to become propertied individuals. There was record of head rights allotted to free Africans who had purchased and transported servants of their own: "In 1664, Anthony and Mary Johnson appear in the Northampton court records, two of the 62 Africans listed among the 450 odd 'tithables' on the tax lists." The simple fact that taxes could be collected from these people indicated that their legal status in-

---

23. As early as March 1662 "it was becoming clear that some Africans were being held to serve for life, rather than for a fixed period." One example of the increasing differences between the African slave and European servant is evident in the laws stipulating punishment of indentured servants for running away with salves: "Bee it enacted That in case any English servant shall run away in company with any negroes who are incapable of making satisfaction by addition of time, Bee it enacted that the English so running away in company with them shall serve for the time of the said negroes absence as they are to do for their owne by a former act" Hening, II, 26.

24. The three most significant laws that define the status of African slaves come from the Virginia colony—other colonies had similar laws or quickly adopted policies based upon Virginia's acts. The most important features were that children would inherit the slave status through their mothers,[i] that the slave status what a permanent condition (as opposed to indentured time-limited service),[ii] and that slaves would be considered 'real estate.'[iii]

i ACT XII. Negro womens children to serve according to the condition of the mother. 2 Hening (VA) 170 (Dec. 1662).

ii An Act Concerning Negroes & other Slaues. Proceedings and Acts of the General Assembly (1664). Assembly Proceedings (MD) 533 (Sept. 1664).

iii ACT XXII. An act declaring the Negro, Mulatto, and Indian slaves within this dominion, to be real estate. 3 Hening (VA) 333 (Oct. 1705).

25. Hendrick Veronica Codifying Humanity: The Legal Line between Slave and Servant (2006)13 Texas Wesleyan Law Review Fort Worth.

cluded the right to own property. Furthermore, when "Anthony and Mary reappeared in the historical record, they had four children and claimed 250 acres of land due them for five head-rights of … persons who were indentured servants on their estate."[26] However, in rapid order, the status of the Africans was transmuted into slavery through a series of laws that curtailed the indentured of African servants.

The system evolved into a two track system of bondage: slavery and indenture. Within this division, the indenture system had multiple levels: the voluntary contract workers—represented by Moraley—were most often economically disadvantaged individuals. Moraley himself had once been part of the rising English middle class until his dissolute ways and resultant disinheritance propelled him into a state of destitution. In order to rectify his situation, Moraley gambled on life in the colonies where he hoped to make his fortune after his fulfilling his contract.

The second group of voluntarily bound servants was called Redemptioners and they often had economic support or highly valuable skills with which to trade for passage, garnering short indenture contracts and better conditions in transit and upon arrival. Redemptioners usually traveled in families and intended to repay their travel debts upon arrival in the colonies; this group was represented by Alice in Gunning's *Bound*. The third group of indentured servants was composed of convicts. The transportation of British convicts to the colonial shores of America was supported by England through a £5 fee given to particularly favored captains. Sending convicts to the colonies had a twofold advantage: the prisons were emptied—thereby removing an economic drain as well as an undesirable element from society—and the developing colony was provided with a cheap form of labor. Cot Quashey's experience portrayed in McCafferty's *Testimony* paralleled the structure of this system. Although not convicted of a crime or held in prison prior to her transport to the colonies, she was captured and bound to service in the same manner and under the same oversight as the imprisoned convicts.[27]

The time about which Moraley wrote was a period when the American colonies were in desperate need for labor. This desperation was reflected

---

26. See the National Park Service (NPS), U.S. Department of the Interior website for other court cases involving slaves: http://www.cr.nps.gov/ethnography/aah/aaheritage/Chesapeake_furthRdg2.htm.

27. Many of the convicts in this system had been erroneous charged and imprisoned. There is evidence that the intent of such incarceration was mercenary and the results were exploitative.

in the increasingly generous head rights[28] offered to individuals responsible for bringing laborers to the colonies. Similarly, the Freedom Dues granted to indentured servants upon completion of their contracts increased as the demand for labor became fierce. In conjunction with the growing demand for laborers in the expanding colonial settlements came a decline in the number of European laborers willing to enter into indentured servitude. Ultimately, these changes propelled the African slave trade, which became the primary source of labor in the colonies by the mid-1800s.[29]

However in the earlier period, indentured servitude was a standard method for socially and economically disadvantaged European individuals to better their prospects. Although illness and death were frighteningly common occurrences on the passage from Europe, as related in *Bound*, and many individuals perished upon arrival to the colonies, indentured servitude was looked upon as a viable way to escape the hardships caused by the failing European economies.[30] It is important to note that servants were not simply desperate to escape from dire circumstances at home; many endeavored to create prosperous futures in their new homeland. Robert O. Heavner noted that many servants signed indentures for the strict purpose of learning to read and write.[31] Others took the view that their

---

28. As a financial reward, all employers who brought new workers to the colonies were granted land or other goods. These rewards based upon the number of imported people, or 'heads,' became known as 'head rights.' Fifty acres of land, or sometimes one hundred acres in Maryland, were paid to anyone who paid a person's passage to the colony.

29. The slave trade expanded rapidly as masters recognized the ultimate profitability of perpetually slavery over that of term labor. Not only were the African slaves held in bondage for life, which quickly compensated for their higher initial cost, but children born of slaves would increase the masters' property holding. Additional qualities specific to the Africans contributed to their exploitation: a primary issue was the inability of slaves to return to their homelands. Additionally, the lack of English language skills, family or community connections, and geographic awareness limited the ability of slaves to first escape and then maintain independence outside of the slave system.

30. Heavner, R.O. 1978, "Indentured Servitude: The Philadelphia Market, 1771–1773", The Journal of Economic History, vol. 38, no. 3, pp. 701–713. Heavner notes that several factors converged to establish the contracts of indentured servants: "master and servant met in a market, and … the servant trade was an accepted part of the labor scene of Colonial America. Laws, prices, terms, and contract provisions were not the result of haphazard events but of purposive economic behavior" (713).

31. Heavner sites a colonial observer Peter Kaim, who described the pattern of German indentured servants as contracting themselves for the specific purpose of language acquisition: "'Many of the Germans who come hither, bring money enough with them to pay their passage, but rather suffer themselves to be sold, with a view

indenture was on a par with the apprentice system from which they would gain knowledge and experience in a valuable trade through their contracts. Those who already possessed a trade hoped to use the period of indenture to establish a business reputation and create a solid clientele. In keeping with these perspectives, Moraley's original intentions were to profit from his experience as both a watchmaker and an educated man and to bring these skills to bear in the New World. Certainly, it seemed that Moraley had the necessary skills to situate himself in Pennsylvania and that his failure to do so came more from his lack of industry than lack of chance.

Moraley experienced relative ease and freedom upon arrival in the colonies, contrary to what the law proscribed and different from the accounts seen in fictional and historical narratives. As part of the indentured servant contract, which was often a simple standardized form with blank spaces left for the servant's name and length of contract, were a series of restrictions to which the servants agreed. For example, marriage was disallowed by the terms of most contracts.[32] Similarly, if a male servant was proven to be responsible for a pregnancy, additional time would be added to his contract to compensate for loss of his labor and productivity. The logic ran that the servant would expend time and energy to support and/or care for his child. As noted earlier, if a female servant became pregnant, her time would be extended to compensate for the reduction of profit due to her limited work ability during her pregnancy as well as the costs of medical attention for herself and her child. A woman's contract could be extended anywhere from one year to three.

One of the more disagreeable aspects of indentured servitude was the variable length of contract time directly related to value of one's labor. If servants were able to earn high rates, then the contract would be short. Although this often proved to be an equitable situation, at times the con

---

that during their servitude they may get some knowledge of the language" in Peter Kaim, "Travels in North America," in Douglass C. North and Robert Paul Thomas, eds., The Growth of the American Economy to 1860 (Columbia, SC., 1968), p. 117. Heavner goes on to explain that "those German servants who specifically contracted to be taught English were in many cases not penniless" (710).

32. March 1642–3: "Be it enacted and confirmed by this Grand Assembly that what man servant soever hath since January 1640 or hereafter shall secretly marry with any mayd or woman servant without the consent of her master or mistress if she be a widow, he or they so offending shall in the first place serve out his or their tyme or tymes with his or their masters or mistresses, and after shall serve his or their master or mistress one compleat year more for such offence committed, And the mayd or woman servant so marrying without consent as aforesaid shall for such her offence double the tyme of service with her master and mistress," Hening, I, 252–253.

ditions of the contract would underestimate the value of labor. Since the negotiation favored the employer rather than the employee, instances of malfeasance were often reported. An example would be contracting a servant as a farmhand then employing him as a blacksmith, a position which was highly valuable and usually contracted for short-term indenture. An additional inequity came in the valuation of labor: backbreaking service in the form of farm work was judged as unskilled labor and therefore earned longer-termed contracts despite its arduousness. What must be reemphasized to understand the conditions of indenture, in contrast to slavery, was that the servants' labor was contracted and owned by the master, not the servants themselves.[33] The indentured servants did, however, agree to tremendous restrictions of their personal freedoms. In addition to the prohibition against marriage and reproduction, laws restricted servants' mobility: during periods when servants ran away in high numbers, a pass was required for a servant to travel far from his or her master's land. Moraley, however, freely roamed from Pennsylvania to New Jersey without incurring significant reprisal. Furthermore, when one work situation proved to be a bad match for both servant and master, Moraley found himself easily transferred to another situation. This contrasted directly with autobiographical accounts of other indentured servants of the period as well as the fictional situations described earlier.

Ultimately, Moraley left this master to wander, to adventure, as he explained it. When Moraley was brought before the magistrate for breach of contract, he was handled gently. This presentation was surprising especially in respect to a separate section in which Moraley decried the mistreatment of servants and the lack of provisions many received. Noting the brutality of reprimand, the lack of proper food and clothing, Moraley explained that contrary to law, masters were allowed to exploit their workers, who had little legal recourse. This complaint against mistreatment seemed more consistent with other reports from indentured servants.

There were two famous letters from servants written to their parents denouncing their situation in servitude and the horrors of indenture in the New World. Servants write to beg aid and money to purchase their freedom. Richard Frethorne's heartbreaking account of his life as a ser-

---

33. The stipulations of the indentured servant contract led to the development of slave codes. For example, an indentured servant promised his or her time, a period of years, rather particular product or skill. During this phase, the servant's time was owned, closely approximating the later development where the servants themselves would be owned.

vant told of malnourishment, illness, and physically impoverished conditions. He also claimed that his master treated him and others with vi-
ciousness and violence. In another equally poignant letter home, a young
woman begged her father for rescue. She too cited the unacceptable, and
unexpected, nature of her indenture, outlining the poverty of her condition and the cruelty of her master. In contrast, Moraley's complaint seems
mild. He states that when "Complaint [is] made to a Magistrate against
the Master for Nonperformance, the Master is generally heard before the
Servant, and it is ten to one if [the servant] does not get his Licks for his
Pains, as I have experienced upon the like Occasion, to my Cost."[34] Even
though Moraley grumbled about an unfair system of rights, he nonetheless fared well in the incident detailing his escape and return to his master. The outcomes reported by other indentured servants lament
maltreatment and erratic legal support despite that a system of law was
"effected a compromise to protect master's property rights and to provide
humane treatment for those under bondage."[35, 36] Therefore, Moraley's
experience offered an intriguing, if problematic, view on the system.

Perhaps Moraley's reported experiences reflected the one major distinction between his situation and that of the typical colonial immigrant
servant: Moraley was well-educated. He had had two periods of apprenticeship in England. His first situation was in a law office, and the second
apprenticeship was for his own father, a watchmaker. Therefore, before a
series of unfortunate occurrences compounded by his self-acknowledged
idle ways, Moraley's social position seemed secure. These advantages translated to the conditions of his tenure in the American colonies, and his
service was relatively easy.[37]

---

34. Moraley, 61.

35. "Included were laws setting term lengths and working hours, laws requiring
the payment of 'freedom dues to released servants, and laws prescribing term extensions for servants who ran away or bore children" (Klepp, 207).

36. The 1934 Bulletin of the Business Historical Society's details Labor Agreements
and Indentures with an example of an agreement which reads, the servant "shall not
waste the goods of his said Master, nor lend them unlawfully to another. At cards, dice
or any other unlawful game, he shall not play. He shall not absent himself, by day or
by night from the service of his said master, without leave; nor haunt or frequent ale-
houses, taverns or gaming places. He shall not contract matrimony within the said
term; nor shall he commit any acts of vice or immortality which are forbidden by the
Laws of Commonwealth" (106).

37. One question remains is why Moraley receives a 5 year contract rather than a
shorter term which reflected his work skills and his educational experiences.

Although many things in Moraley self-report were suspicious, he was, in fact, born into a financially secure family with strong social connections. Moraley stated, "My Parents were of no mean Account, and in good Circumstances, my Father being the third and youngest Son of a Gentleman, chief of an ancient Family and considerable Estate, descended from the Barons *Morley*, of *Swanton Morley*, in *Norfolk*."[38] Moraley took great pains to reassure his readers that his current status as an indentured servant was due to circumstances beyond his personal control. His family suffered a dramatic financial blow due to investments in what came to be known as the South Sea Company "bubble." Moraley claimed his father lost £800[39] on this venture alone. Not long after this devastation, Moraley's father died leaving him bereft of his apprenticeship and his direct inheritance.

Although the paternal death dramatically altered Moraley's standing, his mother's remarriage was what Moraley points to as his personal ruin. Again, under the laws of *coverture*, upon her remarriage, Moraley's mother would have had her financial accounts transferred to that of her husband. Although portions of her inherited estate may have remained in her legal control, it was unclear how much practical control she had over assets. Nonetheless, Moraley's own inheritance should have been protected; however, Moraley explained to his readers that he was cut off from his legacy by an uncaring mother and left without resource or support. This, he alleged, inspired him to adventure to the colonies in search of his fortune. Although these descriptions were the basis of a good yarn,[40] Moraley had certainly stretched the truth to accommodate his literary agenda which was to create a sympathetic readership and promote his social status in England in preparation for his return.

In commenting upon Moraley's credibility, the modern editors of his autobiography highlighted supplemental information which, in contrast to his self-report, may have been the actual events impelling Moraley to America:

---

38. Moraley, 5.

39. This valued converted to the US dollar and adjusted from the year 1720 to 2006 would approximate $47,000. Calculate Consumer Price Index (CPI) from 1665–2012 http://www.austintxgensoc.org/calculatecpi.php.

40. The editors suggest that "Moraley's memoir can be compared to contemporary fictional accounts, especially the novels of Daniel Defoe, including Robinson Crusoe (1719) and The Fortunes and Misfortunes of the Famous Moll Flanders (172) ... Aphra Behn, Oroonoko; or the Royal Slave (1696) and Joseph Addison, Cato: A Tragedy (1713)." xxxix.

Moraley is more likely to omit significant events than he is to lie. This is especially true of the period between the remarriage of his mother on October 19, 1728 (three years after the death of his father), and his decision to sell himself into servitude a year later. Upon remarriage, Moraley's mother, like all married women, lost control of her property to her spouse—her new lord and master.[41]

The editors then listed several reasons which may have influenced the financial decisions of the new household and concluded with the comment that "Moraley was cast adrift, quickly became impoverished, and soon landed in Newcastle's Newgate Prison as an insolvent debtor—an incident that he fails to mention in his autobiography."[42] Moraley's time spent in debtors' prison, compounded by his earlier admissions of being a spendthrift when he "did little else but vapour about the Streets"[43] instead of studying, weigh against him. Therefore, what can be gleaned from Moraley's version of events was his desire to paint himself as a clever adventurer who was buffeted by the cruel winds of fortune rather than a spendthrift who was sent to the colonies for his bad debts. At the same time that Moraley endeavored to create a rogue-like persona in hopes that his memoir would sell widely, he also attempted to create a pitiable persona deserving of aid upon his return to England. However, due to his self-descriptions, the reader was more apt to condemn him for his slovenly ways and impugn him for theft, breach of contract, and incorrigibly lying.

One of the first events that Moraley presents in a rather offhanded fashion was his theft of raisins aboard the ship to America. He said, "in the Afternoon, the Master and Mate being absent, I ventur'd into the Cabin, and peeping into a Chest, discovere'd a large Quantity of Raisins, of which I made free with about two Pound, and pocketed them for my own Use" [original spelling retained].[44] This was presented as mere happenstance, with no apology or further explanation. Nonetheless, in the later part of the text, he stated that "Raisins and Currants are seldom used, by reason of their Dearness, being Twelve-pence a Pound."[45] Since, according to David

41. Moraley, 112.
42. Moraley, 112.
43. Moraley, 9.
44. Moraley, 17.
45. Moraley, 52.

Galenson's[46] estimation, Moraley sold five years[47] of his labor for £9, his theft of 24 pence is no small thing. If he had been caught, he would have been subjected to physical punishment or an extension of his contract time to compensate for the sum. The other aspect in Moraley's history that made this incident particularly interesting was the cause of his incarceration in Newgate Prison: "London officials arrested him on June 23, [1728] leveling the charge of simple grand larceny for the theft of a 'bushel and a half of Wheaten Flour.' [When] his case came to trial at the court of Old Baily on July 9, Moraley won acquittal, [because] 'the Evidence against the prisoner not being Sufficient.' "[48, 49, 50] It was difficult to judge whether Moraley was simply reporting the ship event because he found it amusing or if he felt the need to alert the reader to his penchant for theft. In any case, the fact that he became a defendant in a criminal proceeding for the theft of wheat, and yet blithely reports his theft of raisins, indicated that his concern for personal improvement in the colonies was suspect.

A second interpretation may be that Moraley felt a certain confidence that he would be able to maneuver out of difficult circumstances. It seems that he had a knack for circumventing the law. Many problematic situations which Moraley reports escaping are experienced far differently by

---

46. Galenson provides a clear overview of the prices paid at auction for indentured servants arriving to the colonies. He explains that "all servants who migrated to America incurred debts of similar value ... passage charges were uniform for all servants, and maintenance costs and Freedom Dues varied little across individuals. As a result, every servant contract was a promise to repay approximately the same sum of money" (449). What differed from servant to servant was the value of his or her labor, which was reflected in the length of indenture for which an individual served. Skilled laborers tended to have shorter contracts than unskilled workers. See Galenson, D.W. 1981, "The Market Evaluation of Human Capital: The Case of Indentured Servitude", The Journal of Political Economy, vol. 89, no. 3, pp. 446–467.

47. According to Galenson, the average span of an indentured contract was 4 years (453). Skilled workers usually obtained shorter contracts because of the indenture owners received a higher return on investment: Since Moraley was trained as a watchmaker, in addition to his time spent as a legal clerk, his five year contract is an anomaly.

48. Moraley, 113.

49. Klepp, 113.

50. The transcript reads: "William Morley, of St. Margaret's Westminster, was indicted for feloniously stealing a Bushel and a half of Wheaten Flour, the 23d of June last; but the Evidence against the Prisoner not being sufficient, he was acquitted." Old Bailey proceedings, "William Morely," July 9, 1729 Old Bailey Ref: t17290709-40 at www.oldbaileyonline.org accessed December 17, 2006.

other indentured servants. Again, Richard Frethorne's 1623 letter to his parents described a situation far different from that of Moraley's. Frethorne begged his parents to rescue him from his indenture through any means available to them. He suggested ways in which either they can borrow the money or he himself might be able to earn the money in order to buy out his contract. He bemoaned his situation, saying, "I have nothing to comfort me, nor is there nothing to be gotten here but sickness and death, except [in the event] that one had money to lay out in some things for profit. But I have nothing at all—no, not a shirt to my back but two rags."[51] The difference between Frethorne and Moraley, in part, may stem from the different periods of their servitude—over one hundred years. Also contributing to the contrast in their situations was the type of labor they offered their masters: Frethorne was an example of an unskilled worker living outside of Jamestown, Virginia in the early colonial period. Nonetheless, Frethorne's reportage was more in keeping with the overall experiences of indentured servants in the Americas. In fact, the ill treatment which indentured servants received was noted as a contributing factor to the declining participation in the indenture system.

Therefore, the relative freedom with which Moraley changed masters or abandoned his master entirely was an anomaly. Although these events do not speak well of Moraley's character—he continued his story with tales of drinking and petty behavior—the key issue was the lack of legal reprisal for these events. Initially, Moraley desired to live in Philadelphia and asked his master to sell his indenture to someone in Philadelphia. Although it was common for indentured servants' contracts to be sold, it was required that they remain in the same province. Since Moraley's indenture was originally purchased in Burlington, New Jersey, he was unable to transfer to a master in Philadelphia. Laws of different provinces followed the 1682 "Great Law" passed in Chester, which stated "that no master or mistress or freeman of the Province or the Territories thereunto belonging, shall presume to sell or dispose of any servant into any other Province."[52] This law was followed up by the act of 1700, which prevented and discouraged servants from leaving the province of Pennsylvania, and contained the provision "that no Indentured Servitude servant bound to serve in this province, or Counties annexed, shall be sold or disposed of to any person residing in any other Province or government'" (Geiser 1901). Despite these legal

---

51. Moraley, 36.
52. Geiser, 78.

prohibitions, Moraley, impatient and unsatisfied with his master's refusal to transfer his indenture, ran away.

After being caught, Moraley recounted that he was imprisoned, released, and reconciled with his master. He suffered no penalty despite that fact that by law his master was entitled to add two years to Moraley's contract. The typical punishment for an absentee was "for every day they shall soe absent themselves, serve twenty eight days to their master or mistresse, over and above the contracted tyme of servitude."[53] As the rate of escape increased throughout the colonies, so did the penalties. One law read that for "every naturall day" an indentured servant remained absent, they were required to "'serve one whole weeke, and for every weeke, if they shall att any one tyme soe long absent themselves, one whole year ... over and above their contracted tyme.'"[54] Furthermore, a 1744 "provision was made for whipping escaped servants [and remanding them to] hard labor for thirty days."[55] According to such laws, Moraley's treatment was extremely gentle. He explains that his master forgave his punishment of a two-year increase in his servitude contract and comments upon the generosity of his master, saying, "I was ever after perfectly pleased with my Master's Behaviour to me, which was generous."[56]

Significantly, only two groups are absent from Moraley's tale of slavery and servitude: enslaved Native Americans and indentured convicts. However, during this period of colonial expansion both forms of bound labor would have been highly visible. The colonial campaign against the native population took three basic forms: assimilation, incarceration, and eradication. Nonetheless, Moraley's descriptions of the native people of Delaware, the Lenape, is a romanticized version which the editors of his narrative attribute to the fact that "many Europeans" developed an idealistic attitude "as the Native American population declined along the eastern seaboard and no longer posed a substantial threat."[57] After detailing quaint habits, perhaps gleaned through conversation rather than observation,

---

53. Smith, 74.
54. Smith, 74.
55. Smith details the corporal punishment for servants: Dennis Mahoon was sentenced to "be stripped naked to his Waste & receive thirty nine lashes upon his naked back." Another servant, Philip Orrill, receive twenty-on lashes refusing to observe his mistress's lawful commends. See Smith, W.B. 1961, White Servitude in Colonial South Carolina, University of South Carolina Press, Columbia.
56. Moraley, 82.
57. Moraley, 63.

Moraley boldly stated that "there is always a perfect Agreement [which] subsists between the English and" the Lenape. This final statement indicated Moraley's ignorance of the colonial governments' enslavement of the native population. The fact was that, early on, there was an interest in using Native Americans as slaves. However, the colonists soon came to believe that Africans tended to be more reliable and more profitable than the Native American Indians. This was due partly to the fact that the Indians knew the area so well that escape was relatively easy for them and once gone they were almost impossible to find, and partly to the fact that the Indians were especially susceptible to European disease resulting in the early death of many of them. Increasingly, the colonists came to hold onto their African slaves while shipping their Indian slaves to Barbados for resale. As the use of African slaves increased, the use of indentured servants declined, ultimately discontinuing entirely.

With respect to the indenture of convicted felons coming from England, it is very likely that Moraley avoided their representation due to his personal experiences at Newgate Prison. Perhaps he avoided this group so that his own incarceration would remain unconnected to his tenure as an indentured servant. Nonetheless, the oversight is noticeable. Farley Grubb stated that "approximately 50,000 British convicts were sentenced to servitude and forcibly transported to America between 1718 and 1775" and that "they represented roughly a quarter of all British arrivals and half of all English arrivals in this period."[58] Since Moraley comments upon various forms of slavery and servitude, it was odd that he skipped creating a tale of adventure to describe an encounter with such an individual. However, the stated purpose of his narrative was to gain the respect—and financial support—of his countrymen upon return to England. Additionally, he might have forgone such a description because his status as an independent indentured servant might have been hard to establish in his readers. The slippage between the two groups was common and often these separate clusters were conceived as one entity. Grubb went on to describe the normalcy of convict indentures, stating that "shippers carried both indentured and convict servants on the same voyage" and "while under contract in America indentured and convict servants were largely indistinguishable."[59] Therefore, instead of telling the tale of a scallywag, Moraley decided to fill his text with a tale of piracy and kidnapping.

---

58. Grubb, 94.
59. Grubb, 95.

The adventures of Alonso Tellez de Alemenara referred to as "The Fortunate Andalousian" take up a chapter of Moraley's autobiography. Moraley relays the fictitious experiences of a well-to-do Spaniard who is captured by Barbary pirates and sold into slavery. Alemenara explains that after the ship was plundered, the crew was "secured under Hatches, and the Ship steered its course for Sallee,[60] a Piratical Port in the Atlantick Ocean … After some time we were set on shore, in order to be presented to the King of Morocco, all slaves brought into his Ports, being his Property."[61] In this brief account, the Andalousian told first of the harsh conditions in which a "chain of twenty three Pounds Weight"[62] was fastened about his legs. He then told of his slow progress up the ranks of slaves. After a disastrous military campaign, Alemenara obtained "the King's Favor, and was awarded to the Post of Receiver of the Taxes."[63] Through this advancement, Alemenara was not only able to lose his chains, but was also able to "secure about forty Pounds Weight"[64] of gold and eventually escaped from his captors entirely. Although Moraley's rendition of the tale of piracy and forced slavery was certainly fictitious, it was based upon some factual accounts and reflected in the laws and acts against piracy, abduction, and enslavement of European travelers. Marcus Rediker noted that "the Anglo-American pirates active between 1716 and 1726[65] occupied a grand position in the long history of a robbery at sea. Their numbers, near five thousand, were extraordinary, and their plundering was exceptional in both volume and value."[66] In fact Galenson noted that there were over three thousand indentured servants' records kept at the Guildhall in London to insure that merchants who transported minors across the sea for labor were safe "from

---

60. "Located on the Atlantic cost of Morocco, Salé was a noted center for the corsairs" (Moraley, 38).

61. Moraley, 38.

62. Moraley, 38.

63. Moraley, 39.

64. Moraley, 39.

65. As a side note, it is interesting to remember that Miguel de Cervantes Saavedra and his brother were captured by Barbary pirates and ransomed back to their family. Although the brother was released somewhat expeditiously, Cervantes remained in captivity for five years. The experiences of his life among the Moors in Algiers would have contributed to his anti-Muslim sentiments found in his masterpiece, Don Quixote. A similar negative sentiment can be found in Moraley's text in relation to all non-Christians. See Hendrick, Veronica "Cervantes and Servitude: Competing Histories and the Treatment of the Poor." SCSU Press, New Haven, CT. November, 2005.

66. Rediker, 203.

prosecution for kidnapping."[67] By presenting the story of Alemenara, Moraley helped to establish his own respectability: Implicit in the tale was the correlation between Alemenara's ill fortune and Moraley's own hard luck. Equally important was the fact that Alemenara established himself, through the aid of friends and supporters, as a successful businessperson. Through this tale Moraley hoped to lure his own supporters and financial security.

The stories of kidnapping, slavery, and indentured servitude described in Moraley's *The Infortunate* gave the modern reader access into the lives of various servants in the 18th century British colony of Pennsylvania. Furthermore, Moraley's descriptions of his personal experiences highlighted the economic and legal conditions in England which propelled thousands to enter into indentured contracts. And embedded in Moraley's renditions of other servant and slave stories were legal actions and policies. For example, the stories of kidnapping and forced labor touched upon the problem of piracy and enslavement of Europeans. Equally important were the representations of the colonial system of slavery which preyed upon Africans. The lack of legal protections for this last group—and the resulting maltreatment the African slaves received—were of particular concern for Moraley. Therefore, although Moraley's quirky tale was certainly suspect, and its literary merits were questionable, it is a useful document for analyzing a firsthand account of an indentured servant in America. It also provides a point of reference when investigating the purely fictional accounts of indenture offered by modern writers such as McCafferty and Gunning.

---

67. In his article, "British Servants and the Colonial Indenture System in the Eighteenth Century," Galenson states that "This set of indenture papers owes its existence to a clause of an act of Parliament of 1717 designed to protect the English merchants who signed servants to indentures. The clause made it lawful for merchants to transport minors provided the potential servants were brought before a magistrate of London, or two magistrates elsewhere, in order to acknowledge that they went of their own accord" (42).

Chapter Five

Native American Enslavement and Other Legalized Brutality

When searching through the documents related to slavery and the abolitionist movement, as well as narratives reflecting these events in American history, one story line remained conspicuously underrepresented: namely, that at one stage of our history, there were several thousand slaves who were not Africans but Native Americans. Similarly, contemporary fiction focusing upon Native Americans seemed to have completely elided this reality. Moreover, the power of this inherently rich subject matter suggested that its underrepresentation was due to a lack of awareness. The causes for the general neglect of Native American enslavement fall into multiple categories: pre-colonial Native American systems of slavery, gender bias, perceptions of slavery as an African-only experience, racial blending of enslaved populations, clerical errors in the tracking of Native American slaves, and Native American silence. These factors culminated in abridged representation of Native Americans as slaves. However, enslavement was an ongoing condition imposed upon Native Americans from their earliest encounter with European powers.

The impact of slavery on Native Americans can be seen in connection with the history of broken treaties, which brutalized native populations. These issues coincided with the rise of the African slavery system and the fall of the indentured servant system in early America. Several problematic issues quickly presented themselves when discussing the enslavement of native peoples, the most significant of which was the scanty references to Native American slaves in literary narratives. The reason for this dearth of literary imagining connected to the relatively impoverished historical chronicles of Native Americans in early America. The factor influencing, if not causing, the previous two issues was the difficulty of documenting experiences of a preliterate society. Therefore, representations of Native

American slavery in American Literature were overshadowed by other instances of legalized brutality.

The underexplored history of the Native American slave trade was intertwined with that of Africans in the West Indies. Tony Seybert[1] estimated that the number of Indians enslaved by Europeans "certainly numbered in the tens of thousands." He suggested "an estimated 30,000 to 50,000 Indian captives between 1670 and 1715 [were sold] in a profitable slave trade with the Caribbean, Spanish Hispaniola, and northern colonies." One motivation spurring this trade was an exchange that landed Native Americans in the islands and returned Africans to North American shores. The exchange rate for these slaves fluctuated; however, two or three Native American slaves were required to receive one African slave. The valuation was based upon the belief that Africans made better slaves than the Native Americans. This was in part related to the short lifespan of the Native American slaves and in part related to the greater ease with which Native Americans escaped from captivity in the American colonies.

The capture and enslavement of large numbers of Native Americans in order to complete trade arrangements with the islands spiked in this period. The most expedient method used to achieve this goal was through warfare. European powers used tribal wars to their own advantage and used their Native American allies to capture enemy hostages for sale in the slave markets. Often, various colonial powers orchestrated conflicts to obtain captives to exchange in the West Indies.

Not all such captives, however, were obtained through internal tribal conflicts. In New England during the Pequot Wars and King Phillip's War, also called Metacom's War, some slave-capturing assaults were conducted by British colonial troops. In one of the earliest narratives coming out of the Massachusetts Bay Colony, and the earliest penned by a female writer, was *A Narrative of the Captivity and Removes of Mrs. Mary Rowlandson*, also titled *The Sovereignty and Goodness of God*, which told the tale of a 1675 Native American attack on Rowlandson's fledgling Lancaster community.

In Rowlandson's self-focused presentation of the events surrounding the attack on Lancaster by the Wampanoag Indians, Rowlandson recounted the sorrowful tale of her life in captivity. The omission that the Wampanoag were the same tribe encountered by the first settlers landing in Plymouth, Massachusetts in 1620 and that chief Massasoit, Metacom/King Phillip's

---

1. See Slavery and Native Americans in British North America and the United States: 1600 to 1865.

father, was responsible for the pilgrims' survival was significant in light of Rowlandson's presentation of the events. The alliance between the Wampanoag and the British settlers had been an uneasy one, yet the tribe found the association useful in suppressing the aggression of rival tribes such as the Pequot, Narragansett, and the Mohegan. Relations, however, ruptured after treaty negotiations became thorny and one man, John Samasson, was allegedly murdered by three Wampanoag men.

Samasson was a 'Praying Indian,' which meant that he had converted to Christianity. He was also a graduate of Harvard College and a translator for the Wampanoag. It was suspected that Samasson was murdered for betraying Metacom/King Phillip's confidence and disclosing war activities of the Wampanoag. The upshot of his death was the trial, conviction, and execution of the Wampanoag men suspected of the murder. Although the jury was comprised of both British and Native Americans, Metacom/King Philip believed that the action infringed on his tribal sovereignty. Conflict ensued.

In Rowlandson's account of the attack on Lancaster, which was a truly bloody affair, she accented both the brutality of the marauders as well as the innocence of townspeople and their bucolic activities on the day of the invasion. She omitted, however, the precipitating events of the previous months. A brutal attack by the Lancaster militia and British soldiers, numbering by some estimation to be 1,000 strong, was directed at the winter camp of the Narragansett tribe on November 2, 1675. Problematic in Rowlandson's presentation was first, of course, that she belied the brutality of the militia and then second that she obfuscated the innocent position of the Narragansett who were slaughtered in their winter camp. The Great Swamp Fight, known alternatively as the Great Swamp Massacre, attacked primarily women and children in the company of aged warriors no longer able to fight. The Narragansett tribe was, until this point, a neutral peaceful group. The colonial action was a preemptive strike motivated by the anxiety created by the conflicts with various Native American groups in the area.

The fighting between the Wampanoag and the colonists had been ongoing, and The New England Confederation (a coalition of British colonies that included Plymouth, Massachusetts and New Haven, Connecticut) declared war on the Native Americans on September 9, 1675. The Narragansett, however, had remained outside of the conflict in an uneasy peace until the colonial attack. In total, over three hundred Narragansett died in their undefended camp, with several hundred wounded who had escaped only to die later due to injury and inclement weather. Only then did the

Narragansett join with the Wampanoag in an alliance against the colonists: they joined forces and exacted retribution on the village of Lancaster.

Rowlandson's account was a personal drama, written to extol the virtues of Christianity and share her ordeal with her colonial and European readership in an effort to inspire faith and create support for the colonial conflicts against the native populations. As an exemplar of colonial narratives— Rowlandson's narrative was the top selling in both New England and England—her omissions remained unexposed. In keeping with Rowlandson's perspective were the views of Cotton and Increase Mather.

In Cotton Mather's account of the events at the Great Swamp Fight, the one-sided nature of Rowlandson's views was replicated. In both narratives, the justification of British action was embedded in the designation of the Native Americans as savages, and Mather posited the colonists as instruments of God. Mightily unchristian in his descriptions, Mather described the horror of the events with enthusiastic joy. Noting the individuals attempting to flee from the burning camp, he described both the sight and smell of one poor man struggling to disengage from his flaming blanket. For modern readers, the cruelty exhibited in Mather's words and attitudes were shocking, especially given the fact that Mather was a man of the cloth and noted for his religious treaties, most significantly his 1702 *Magnalia Christi Americana*.

However, it must be remembered that it was Mather's recognition of Spectral Evidence which lead to the demise of accused witches in the Salem witchcraft trials Arthur Miller so wonderfully vivified in *The Crucible*. Although Mather did not support the use of spectral evidence during the witchcraft trials, he aggressively defended the judges who did so after the events transpired. His writings about witchcraft and his descriptions of the bloodletting at the Great Swamp Fight, which he clearly relished retelling, was in keeping with other religious and political figures of the time. The writing of William Bradford, in *Of Plimoth Plantation* (1646) was equally brutal in both description and attitude. Therefore, it was a bitter irony that the connection between Bradford and Mather ran a direct line through the Wampanoag family of Massasoit and connected to the replication of broken treaties and Native American enslavement.

The initial account of Bradford, similarly focused upon the colonial settlement in New England, specifically Plymouth Massachusetts, told of the Mayflower's arrival and the tenuous survival of the first settlers in this Northern area. Several legal documents of seminal importance were generated by these pilgrims to the northern colonies. The first document was the November 11, 1620 Mayflower Compact. This social contract was signed by two groups aboard the *Mayflower*, the religious separatists seeking to establish a new society and the religiously unaffiliated settlers, such as Myles Standish, who was invited because of his military expertise. Because the *Mayflower* had landed far north of its charter's designation, the need for an organized system of rules was pressing. The Mayflower Compact was codified to ensure the pilgrim's survival in the rough northern territory.

The second document was a 1621 Peace Treaty, or Friendship Treaty, signed by William Branford, among others, and Massasoit the Wampanoag sachem, Metacom/King Phillip's father. Although this treaty was honored until Massasoit's death, the alliance, which was an uneasy one, ultimately deteriorated. It did, however, enable the colonists and the Wampanoag to remain peaceful during the Pequot Wars. The Pequot Wars, which began in 1634 and raged until 1638, were in part an outcrop of colonial ambitions and European conflict. As the Dutch and English colonies struggled over trade, primarily the fur trade, their respective tribal allies of the Pequot and the Mohegan became embroiled in conflict. In Bradford's presentation, the actions of the Pequot seem both unprovoked and unfathomable, much like the later presentation of Rowlandson. Bradford, too, described the innocence of the settlers. In righteous retaliation, Bradford explained how the colonials combined with an allied Native American tribes as well as members from the Bay Colony to subdue the querulous Pequot.

Bradford told how friendly "Indians brought them [the colonial soldiers] to a forte of the enemies (in which most of their chief men were) before day" and they "entered the forte with all speed."[2] Bradford detailed the horror that ensued: "They approached the same with great silence, and surrounded it both with English and Indeans, that they might not breake out; and so assualted them with great courage, shooting amongst them, and ... those that first entered found sharp resistance from the enimie, who both shott at and grapled with them."[3] Without guilt he explained that the trapped members of the tribe "rane into their howses, and brought out fire, and sett them on fire, which soone tooke in their matts, and ... all was quickly on a flame, and therby more were burnte to death then was otherwise slain."[4] Bradford's retelling of these events not only exonerated the brutality of the colonial soldiers, but also concealed the blamelessness of their victims.

---

2. Bradford, 338.
3. Bradford, 339.
4. Bradford, 339.

Even as the defeated Native Americans ran to their homes, they were pursued. As the fire swept through the fort, the soldiers were able to pick off the fleeing people piecemeal: "Those that scaped the fire were slaine with the sword; some hewed topeeces, others rune throw with their rapiers, so as they were quickly dispatchte, and very few escaped. It was conceived they thus destroyed about 400."[5] Although Bradford noted that it "was a fearfull sight to see them thus frying in the fyer, and the streams of blood quenching the same,"[6] he, nonetheless, ended his reflection with the belief that this bloody work was condoned by God: "the victory seemed a sweete sacrifice, and they gave the prays therof to God, who had wrought so wonderfuly for them, thus to inclose their enimise in their hands, and give them so speedy a victory over so proud and insulting an enimie."[7] The right-eousness of the colonial soldiers was extoled in Bradford's account.

In response to elisions and instances of bias in writings such as Row-landson's, Mather, and Bradford's, scholars have reconsidered and re-framed their presentations of the Pequot war. Steven Katz explained that "in place of the view that the English were simply protecting themselves by preemptively attacking the Pequots, the revisionists argued that the Europeans used earlier, limited threats against them as cause to bring mass destruction on the Pequots."[8] In his well-balanced piece,[9] Katz outlined both the misdeeds of the Pequots and the reasonable anxiety of the colonials: an uprising in Virginia (1622) had left 350 dead; several conflicts between the Pequot and the settlers had resulted in deaths in both camps; and the Mohegan sachem Uncas[10] had informed his British allies in New England that the Pequot were restless. This backdrop explained why the Puritans decided to quell potential movement of the Pequot. It did not, however, explain why 90 men, under the command of John Endecott, went to Block Island, home of the Narragansett.

The principal source for the Block Island incident is *John Winthrop's Journal, History of New England, 1630–1649,* in which Winthrop detailed John Endecott's orders: Endecott's men were to kill the natives of Block

---

5. Bradford, 338.

6. Bradford, 339.

7. Bradford, 339–40.

8. Katz, 206.

9. Katz is interested in exposing both the bias of early writers and thinkers as well as disarming what he sees as equally erroneous renderings of the Pequot War. In particular, Katz takes to task modern interpretations which see the brutality of the colonists as clearly motivated by a genocidal agenda.

10. Uncas is a character name used in Cooper's The Last of the Mohicans.

Island, sparing the women and children. The fact that the people of Block Island were Narragansett, and not Pequot, was alluded to in passing: Rather than through direct action, the Narragansett were guilty—they were said to have harboured the Pequot men accused of murdering several colonists. The soldiers were told "to spare the women and children, and to bring them away,"[11] perhaps with the intent to enslave them. Winthrop stated that after clearing the island threat, the men should move onto the Pequot and address the murder of Captain Stone.[12] Cave stated that "available documentary evidence indicates that Stone's death was an unexpected consequence of a trading rights squabble between the Dutch and their Indian clients in the Connecticut River valley."[13] He noted that Stone, an Englishman, and his crew were misidentified as Dutch and were killed in retaliation for the Dutch murder of their sachem, Tatobem, for whom the Pequot had paid ransom. Despite this motivation, Stone's death was erroneously billed as an aimless act of Pequot aggression. In an ever-expanding circle of violence, retaliation inspired retaliation.

The death of Captain Stone, as well as several members of his crew, became a rallying call. His death was commonly accepted as the catalyst to Puritan action, even if historians debate the nature of Stone's interaction with the Pequot. Cave explained that "historians sympathetic to the Puritan cause customarily wrote of Pequot 'savagery' and stressed the need to discipline Indians who attacked whites" whereas "historians who deplored the massacre and enslavement of the Pequots, by contrast, pointed to evidence of Stone's bad character and noted that the Massachusetts Bay Colony leaders suspected that he had abused Indians."[14] That such abuse and enslavement were minimized in colonial records was not surprising.

In a similar act of willful ignorance, an attack upon the Pequots was orchestrated despite the fact that Winthrop, in a letter to William Bradford, wrote that the Pequots may be believed when they claim "'they had killed Stone' in a just quarrel."[15] Nonetheless, the colonial soldiers were ordered to demand from the Pequots "one thousand fathom of wampum for dam-

---

11. Winthrop, 186.

12. Citing several sources, including Francis Jennings, Cave states that the "New England's Puritans described John Stone as a drunkard, lecher, braggart, bully, and blasphemer. He was known to have engaged in smuggling as well as privateering. Adding to Stone's unsavory reputation were rumors that he had even resorted to cannibalism while shipwrecked in the Caribbean" (517).

13. Cave, 512.

14. Cave, 518.

15. Cave, 514.

ages, etc., and some of their children as hostages, which if they should refuse," the soldiers should take "by force."[16] Although retribution for murder was understandable, the attack upon the Narragansett, who were guilty only by association, must be perceived as unwarranted aggression.

The war's outbreak coincided with the poorly timed actions of a Native American hunting party which killed several cows and terrified settlers. At the same time as this relatively innocuous blunder, the case of John Stone had become public knowledge. Stone, a confirmed rogue who hailed from the West Indies, was deeply invested in capturing Native American women and children to be sold into slavery. He had been connected to an incident in which Tatobem, the Pequot sachem or paramount chief, had been captured and ransomed back to the tribe. However, instead of embracing the recently ransomed Tatobem, the tribe was only presented with his corpse. In retaliation, an allied tribe of Western Niantic captured and executed Stone, the man they blamed for the murder. These Native American men refused to submit to colonial justice. The subsequent murder of John Oldham, a trapper, further antagonized colonial authorities: a series of raids and battles ensued. The close of the war was brought on by the Mystic Massacre which decimated the Pequot people. At the 1638 Treaty of Hartford, Pequot lands were divided among the victors and the few survivors of the massacre were rendered into slavery.

Almost forty years after the Pequot War, the Narragansett were once again targeted during the King Philip's War despite their acknowledged status of neutrality. Metacom/King Philip was Wampanoag, and it was his tribe that had been embroiled in conflict. Nonetheless, many tribes such as the Narragansett were devastated by the violence which swept through the region.

Much like the historiography of the Pequot War, the assessments of the King Philip War fell into two divergent camps: Philip Ranlet explained that "in the nineteenth century, John Gorham Palfrey stated that King Phillip, chief of the Wampanoag tribe, was 'an unreasoning and cruel barbarian' who had no cause to war against the Puritan settlers."[17] Noting that "Palfrey's attitudes, at times blatantly racist, were not unique among his contemporaries or his predecessors," Ranlet then suggested that historians "arose to champion the cause of the Indians [and have] been accused of sympathizing so totally with the natives that they have failed to appreciate the settlers' experience."[18] The final parallel between these two wars

---

16. Winthrop, 186.
17. Ranlet, 79.
18. Ranlet, 79.

was the gradual buildup of tensions that culminated in massive causalities on both sides and the enslavement of Native Americans.

King Philip's War began in 1675 and lasted for one year. In her well-researched book, *The Name of War: King Philip's War and the Origins of American Identity*, Jill Lepore moved through the events of one of the most vicious conflicts in American history. She contextualized the conflict by suggesting that "New England's Algonquians waged war against the English settlers in response to incursions on their cultural, political, and economic autonomy and, at least in part, they fought to maintain their Indianness," whereas the colonists "waged war to gain Indian lands, to erase Indians from the landscape, and to free themselves of doubts about their own Englishness."[19] With the advent of King Phillip's War, the founding mythology of a peaceful coexistence was dashed. It was replaced with separation and conflict.

One way this conflict manifested itself was over New England trade, including the slave trade. Margaret Ellen Newell noted that "by the mid-18th century, one-third of Indians in southern New England lived in white households as servants or slaves."[20] Combined with the European expansion into native lands, Metacom/King Phillip's leadership was undermined by colonial demands for financial redress. Combined with the various penalties for breaking colonial contracts, Metacom/King Philip responded to the colonial usurpation of his political power. He not only relinquished his guns and autonomy to the colonial magistrates but also was required to do public service and pay financial damages. It is unclear whether he was expected to pay any of his debt in slaves, yet a system of judicial enslavement was in place: "sentencing Native Americans to long periods of involuntary servitude for debt or criminal infraction"[21] was noted by Newell. In fact, all forms of enslavement—whether they resemble servitude, indenture, or life-long slavery—increased after conflicts between Native American and colonial powers, or tribes working in their alliance.

As noted above, one of the first instances of mass Native American enslavement dated back to the Pequot War when many of the remaining members of the vanquished tribe were sold into slavery in Bermuda. The second historically significant enslavement of Native Americans, the sale of Native Americans after King Philip's war, may have been overlooked because it also occurred in Bermuda. Yet, details of slavery practices among

19. Lepore, 8.
20. Newell, 1.
21. Newell, 1.

various Native American tribes appear in Almon Wheeler Lauber's work.[22] Discussing the Pequot slaves, Lauber noted that "forty-eight captives were retained as slaves in the colony"[23] and Guasco stated that "seventeen Pequot Indians—fifteen boys and two women—were ordered to be sent out of New England by Massachusetts officials."[24] The pattern began in 1637 continued until 1677, when Philip's people including his son, were sold to the islands. The removal of Native American slaves from continental America to the Sugar Islands, and as far away as Nicaragua, contributed to the lack of awareness of this part of American slave history.

Just as the Mayflower Compact attempted to establish a method of organization which would bind the disparate individuals to a communal goal, the Wampanoag/Pilgrim Treaty attempted to create a harmonious interchange between foreign entities. Therefore, the erosion of the agreements made in 1620 established unfortunate precedents in the relationship between Native American and European settlers. Metecom/King Phillip's War took on a particularly grim aspect in its retelling by colonial voices.

The complete comfort with which Mather rejoiced in the destruction of the Wampanoag eradicated any sense of a debt owed to these people. Long forgotten was that Metacom/King Phillip's father, Massasoit, and the Wampanoag tribe had insured the survival of the very people who would later slaughter them. Adding insult to injury, after Metacom/King Phillip's death a gruesome artifact in the form of Metacom/King Phillip's head was given to Plymouth and left on display. The death of Metacom/King Philip- was omitted from Mary Rowlandson's narrative as was the utter destruction of his community and his family even though she had been Metacom/King Phillip's captive and was kept among his people.

Metacom/King Phillip's wife and son[25] were sold to the slave trade running from the northern colonies to Barbados but this aspect of the war was absent from these colonial presentations. Just as Mary Rowlandson presented herself and her settlement as innocent so too did other writers

---

22. See Lauber, Almon Wheeler. Indian Slavery in Colonial Times within the Present Limits of the United States, 1913. Despite the date of this work, and that it remained in dissertation form, Lauber's text remains one of the seminal texts investigating Native American slavery.

23. Lauber, 109.

24. Guasco,1.

25. There are discrepancies in reports regarding the fate of King Phillip's wife, Wootonekanuske. In some instances she is reported to have died in captivity and in others she is described as being sold to Barbados.

present Native American conflicts without reference to the culpability of the settlers. The omissions of history in these early narratives, conscious or accidental, was only one of the many reasons for the one-sided perspective about early American and Native American exchange.

Although King Philip's War received scholarly attention, minimal focus had been given to its resultant slavery. Jill Lepore states that *The Narrative of the Captivity and the Restoration of Mrs. Mary Rowlandson* was "considered a foundational work in American literature; it is better remembered than any other account of King Philip's War and is more widely read than any other Indian captivity narrative;" therefore, it can weaken understanding of slavery within the Native American context.[26] Because Rowlandson occluded the reasons for her abduction and portrayed only her own enslavement without reference to similar crimes perpetrated by her people, she eschewed any mention of colonial guilt. She also shunned mention of the enslavement of Native Americans in Massachusetts.

Jill Lepore focused upon this oversight by discussing the enslavement of the captives from the King Philip's War. Specifically, she detailed the enslavement of Philip's young son and the possible enslavement of his wife, Wootonekanuske. In the wake of the war, "at least 180 'heathen Malefactors men, women and Children" were sent aboard the *Seaflower* bound for Bermuda. Although neither mother nor child was on this ship, Lepore quoted a passage from John Cotton's letter to Increase Mather which contains the sentence "Phillips boy goes now to be Sold." She suggested that "Philip's son was finally released from prison, only to be sold into slavery and shipped, most likely to the West Indies."[27] The legacy of Metacom/King Phillip's son's arrival remained part of the Barbadian mythology: many individuals claimed decent from Philip's son or from Wootonekanuske.

Tracing the enslavement of these transported people was more than a little difficult. As Michael J. Jarvis suggested, Bermuda as a colonial locale was relatively absent from analysis: "Neither American nor Caribbean, this ancient British colony has escaped the attention of most colonial historians, a neglect perhaps owing to its small size and anomalous location."[28] Yet, with the arrival of "one Indian and a Negroe" in August 1616, Bermuda gained "the dubious distinction of being the first English colony to import African labor, fully three years before Africans arrived in Virginia."[29]

---

26. Lepore, 125.
27. Lepore, 153.
28. Jarvis, 585.
29. Jarvis, 585.

Bermuda's effacement in the study of slavery contributed to the disregard of Native American slavery.

Barbados and Bermuda were target markets for the sale of Native Americans. The movement of captives from King Philip's War "began early in the war, in the summer of 1675" but "systematic enslavement came on a year later, when large numbers of Indians surrendered or were captured."[30] Regarding the motives for such rapid expansion of the trade in slaves, Lepore noted the following: "colonial authorities hoped the labor provided by Indian servants retained within New England would aid struggling colonists in rebuilding their ravaged towns, while the sale of Indians to foreign slavery would help fill the coffers emptied by wartime expenses."[31] The lucrative slave trade not only created colonial conflict over ownership of the captives, it inspired independent merchants to enter the trade with abandon.

Another reason Native American slavery was understudied related to a gender bias. Because the great majority of Native American slaves remaining in the colonies were women, their enslavement may not have piqued public consciousness. Operating in domestic roles, Native American women could have been considered as typical servants rather than slaves. Those pressed into sexual service were removed from colonial consciousness, and therefore colonial record, for a variety of reasons. The indelicacy of their situation may have contributed to its disregard. Later, in the writing of Harriet Jacobs, whose narrative was discussed earlier, the desire for pure-minded people to shy away from helping victims of sexual abuse was commented upon. In the introduction to her narrative, Jacobs begged the pardon of her readers for her unseemly descriptions. However, Jacobs made it clear that the affront she suffered as a slave woman needed remedy. Since there was no companion voice coming out of Native American slavery, the subject remained hidden.

As evidence of these omissions, Ramsey noted that in South Carolina, "officials never recognized the underlying patterns of the cases that came before them or else considered them unimportant," although these issues inspired Native American aggression.[32] The two items overlooked were "related to the slave trade" and "gender-specific violence." In relation to the captivity narratives following the King Philip's War, Lepore did make

---

30. Lepore, 154.
31. Lepore, 154.
32. par 27.

a gender comparison. She contrasted the captivity of Rowlandson[33] and a man named Joshua Tift, who "was executed—hanged and quartered—for treason."[34] The colonial powers capriciously concluded that Tift had voluntarily stayed with the Narragansett and believed that he fought with them in the Great Swamp battle.

The divergent reception of Rowlandson and Tift may simply be based upon the circumstances of their involvement with their captors: Rowlandson remained in camp throughout the war, while Tift was with the Narragansett during a heated battle. However, Lepore suggested that Rowlandson's gender provided a viable excuse for remaining with her captors, that Tift, "an able bodied man, had little excuse for not violently resisting capture, while Rowlandson, an injured woman carrying an injured infant, had abundant reason to submit."[35] In this case, the enslavement[36] of a woman was forgivable but for a man, it was treasonable.

Beyond the gender bias found in representations of captives, both Native American and colonial, an additional problem with reporting contributed to the lack of narratives reflecting Native American slavery. Despite the corrective approach that has been applied to understanding colonial encounters with native peoples, a problematic situation remains due to the lack of self-representation. Works like *Black Elk Speaks* remain compromised because as Black Elk was speaking, John Neihardt was writing, translating, and editing. Suspect though this narrative may be, the lack of earlier similar samples of Native American thinking can only be viewed as an unfortunate and regrettable fact. Not only did this lack preclude deep understanding of situations from Native American perspective, it resulted in a further gap in both narrative representation and historiography. The replication of these gaps compounded the scenario so completely that the narrative history of Native American slavery was underdeveloped.

---

33. One of Rowlandson's master, Quinnapin, was "tried and found guilty and summarily executed" and Weetamoo, Rowlandson's former 'mistress'… drowned in a river while attempting to escape the English and later had her head cut off and placed on a pole" (Lepore, 155).

34. Lepore, 133.

35. Leopre, 132.

36. Again, the application of the term slave is problematic. Lepore herself notes that "The people who suffered forms of bondage during King Philip's War were called by many names: captives, servants, slaves … during King Philip's war these three terms were sometimes used interchangeably" (135).

In telling the Native American experience from the outside, writers such as Thomas Berger filled the void. Through his rollicking tales of the Cheyenne people in *Little Big Man*, 1964, Burger used the voice of Jack Crabb to narrate the demise of the Cheyenne. The lack of Native American writers accepted or published by mainstream publishers may explain part of the problem and may also explain why Berger's text became so popular. What was unique about this novel was not that it detailed the problematic issues experienced by Native Americans but that it did this through the eyes of settler boy, Jack Crabb, adopted into the Cheyenne tribe.

Jack Crabb witnessed the events that affected the Cheyenne people from both inside the tribe and from the periphery as a member of the US military. He told of the violation of treaties, the rupture of law, the brutal actions of the military and the despicable aspects of Western values. Brilliantly, the novel parallels issues of sexuality, love, friendship, alliances, allegiance, and hatred between the two groups. In each case, Crabb's experiences of the Native Americans was remembered as untarnished and uncompromised whereas Crabb's encounters with the American model were confused or tainted with compromise.

Problematic for the purpose of analyzing the condition of Native American literary accounts was not that Berger had no Native American heritage, although this posed problems for essentialists; it was instead that Crabb functioned as a spokesperson for the Cheyenne. Adopted as a youth by Chief Old Lodge Skins, Crabb had a Forest Gump-like encounter with American History. He learned to gamble and shoot from Wyatt Earp, met Annie Oakley, served General Custer his tea, and acted as a scout at the Battle of Little Big Horn. As a youth growing into manhood, he alternated between Cheyenne and settler identities. At the close of his 107 years, it was clear that his time among the Cheyenne was what he valued most. Despite the century of history recounted by Crabb, roughly paralleling Vine Deloria's time parameters in his text *A Century of Dishonor*, both the enslavement of Native Americans and their exploitation as laborers or military forces was left unexamined and unrepresented. Instead, writers like Berger focused upon the destruction of community caused by westward expansion, broken treaties, forced removal, and the reservation system.

Comment upon the use and misuse of Native American troops was relegated to the writing of novelists such as James Fennimore Cooper. In *The Last of the Mohicans*, Cooper attempted to present figures like Uncas and Chingagook in the most positive light; however, his portrayal was fully ensconced in the thinking of his age and concepts such as the Nobel Savage took center stage in his characterizations. Leaving aside Cooper's Romanization of the Native American scouts Uncas and Chingagook, as well as the equally stereotypical development of the sinister warrior represented by Magua, Cooper presented the use of Native American troops on either side of the French American war in legal terms. Penned in 1826, *The Last of the Mohicans* harkened back to 1757 and the pre-revolutionary context of the French and Indian War. Cooper's presentation showed the French reliance upon the Oneida, and Huron—or Magua as Hawkeye calls the enemy—and the British employment of the Mohicans and Delaware. Embedded in the struggles of the villain, a disgraced Huron who went by various names ranging from the insulting Magua to the French coined "Le Subtil," was the conflicting system of laws and sensibilities represented by Huron and British codes of conduct and their enforcement of law.

At issue, and the root of the novel's plot, was Magua's need for vengeance against the leader of the British forces at Fort Henry, an outpost not far from Albany, NY. Colonel Munro, an historically accurate figure, caused irreparable harm to Magua. The basic conflict stemmed from a moment in which Colonel Munro established that any Native American found intoxicated would be severely punished and publicly humiliated. Therefore, when Magua overindulged in the alcohol shared with the Native American scouts, he drunkenly walked through the soldiers' camp ultimately stumbling upon Munro's tent. The following morning, in front of all those assembled, Magua was stripped to the waist and whipped. Magua's embarrassment was so great that he left the British camp swearing to take vengeance upon all the British and on Monroe in particular.

What was significant about this moment, beyond the plot device it provided, was the misunderstanding between the two groups, the British soldiers and the Native Americans. Munro had no understanding of the disgrace to which he had subjected Magua. The fact that Magua had been physically assaulted was a lesser issue than the fact that he had been humiliated. In sharing his feelings later on in the text, Magua displayed multiple scars he received in battle. With pride he explained where and when each wound was received. However, Munro's whip wounds that turned to scars upon Magua's back were hidden in shame. Munro had no awareness that his actions against Magua would create such bitterness and engender such hatred. Similarly, Magua did not know how to navigate the contradictory situation of being provided alcohol by the soldiers and then being commanded to remain sober. This was one example of the way in which Cooper introduced conflicting concepts of law and justice into his narrative. Much larger issues of war and alliances took up the bulk of the work and echoed the problematic relationships between rising colonial powers and their Native American allies.

Moving to the post-colonial experience of the American and the Native American people is particularly interesting in relation to the laws. Often ignored by literary imaginations was the legacy of the enslavement of Native American populations and the active involvement of several tribes in the slave trade. More often the literary accounts reflected upon the laws related to the rights of native people, their status as residents rather than citizens, with focus upon the land rights, forced marches, religious coercion, and relocation. Bridging the gap were many of the laws of the colonial period that had a direct bearing upon the later development of the reservation system.

Black Elk, and other Native American voices such as Sitting Bull and Crazy Horse, connect to the work of modern Native American writers and their presentation of native populations' experiences with law. Just as Thomas Berger's *Little Big Man* presented a searing representation of the contradictory laws of the 1870s, other works look at the inconsistent aspects of the Jackson administration. For example, The Trail of Tears, the term given to the forced march of the native people across the Mississippi river to the lands designated as Indian Territory, was a particularly common event referred to within the body of Native American writing, but it was told right alongside of tales of westward expansion.

Various economic, social, and political pressures led to the removal of Cherokee, Muscogee/Creek, Seminole, Chickasaw, and Choctaw tribes from the southeastern states, most infamously Georgia. Equally important were the established laws meant to protect the native people and the ways in which these laws were altered, misinterpreted, or ignored for the benefit of the American settlers. These pressures paralleled the conditions that led to the enslavement of Native Americans and to the shortage of literary representations of these events.

Contributing to the under-investigation of the Native American presence in the European slave trade were the existing systems of pre-colonial slavery. Prior to the colonial presence in the Americas, Native Americans commonly enslaved enemies defeated in battle.[37] However, the European demand for labor[38] engendered profiteering in the slave markets, and many tribes embraced this mechanism to increase their wealth, to obtain dom-

---

37. Seybert, 1.

38. British settlers, especially those in the southern colonies, eagerly purchased or captured Native Americans to use as forced labor in cultivating tobacco, rice, and indigo.

inance over neighboring groups, and to create alliances with Spanish, French, or British powers. Michael Guasco noted that recent "historians have effectively reconceptualized Indian slavery as a normative institution with its own parameters which ought to be distinguished from the chattel slavery practiced by Europeans."[39] For example, before the arrival of these European powers, Native American slavery was small in scale and many of the enslaved held social positions within their host community.

Lauber explained the multitudinous ways in which an individual became enslaved. Some were as banal as debt. Gamblers, he said, "not infrequently staked themselves to serve as slaves in case of loss."[40] Depending upon the amount owed, such slavery could last only one year[41] or it could be a life condition that seemed to function much like an indentured servant contract. Lauber notes that in times of financial hardship, as in the "case of famine, the Indians even sold their children to obtain food"[42] but most cases of slavery resulted from defeat in battle.[43]

The forms of slavery—the tasks, duties, as well as the privileges of the Native American slaves—were by no means uniform throughout North America, nor were they consistent by region or group. Nonetheless, it was common for enslaved women and men to preform labor related to the maintenance of their master's household. In some cases, unmarried women and girls functioned in a form of concubinage. James F. Brooks suggest that "rape of female slaves by male slave owners may be the one trans-historical invariant across all cultures" in Native American systems of slavery.[44] However, in many instances, female slaves married members of the tribe. The diverse cultural groups developed unique practices, and their treatment of slaves shifted according to region. In the northwest, Lauber asserts, slavery had "existed for a sufficient length of time before the coming

---

39. Guasco, 3.

40. Lauber, 25.

41. The application of the term slavery is problematic when referring to a time-limited period of bondage; perhaps, here the system is more on par with that of indentured servitude.

42. Lauber, 25.

43. Lauber explains warfare enabled the Iroquois, for example, to hold "both Indians and whites in personal slavery" (29). From Ohio alone, slaves numbered in the hundreds. The Iroquois enslaved the Shawnee and the Miami, to the latter they promised to exchange captured warriors for a quantity of beaver skin but reneged after receiving the goods. Iroquois' slave raids extended into Maryland, Erie, the Carolinas, and Florida.

44. McLemee, 14.

of the whites to modify materially the habits and institutions of the people" leading to rank and cast systems in the region.[45] Building upon the northeastern tribes' systems of rank, the Europeans were able to first utilize, and then later exploit the pre-existence of Native American slavery in the colonies. The existing hierarchal structure allowed the Europeans to point to an established slave class as a justification for enslaving the indigenous peoples of the Americas. These factors limited colonial concern about Native American slavery thereby contributing to underrepresentation of its occurrence.

Similarly, the rationalization for the harsh form of European slavery may have depended upon anecdotal evidence of brutality within the Native American system of slavery. Reports from French settlers cite extreme examples such as slaves who "were forced to eat one of their own nation"[46] as a punishment and a warning to other slaves to maintain correct decorum.[47] Also noted were brutal practices used to prevent slaves from escape, such as "cutting away a part of the foot, or ... cutting the nerves and sinews just above the ankle or instep."[48] The colonial claims of widespread Native American cruelty toward their slaves enabled the settlers to consider the European system of slavery as more compassionate. In many cases, Europeans argued that enslavement could offer redemptive and rehabilitative benefits to their captives.

The Europeans ignored the Native American practice of incorporating captured warriors from enemy tribes into their own group. Within Native American slavery, slaves could transform their status through marriage. Lauber states that women "often preferred to adopt captives into their families to replace lost husbands and sons, rather than to revenge themselves for the loss of relatives by demanding the torture and death of the slaves."[49] European depictions of Native American enslavement ignored these social promotions and instead focused upon the executions of slaves deemed too sick or too problematic. Cherry-picking the tenets of Native American slavery in this way allowed the colonists to misrepresent the differences between the two systems of slavery.

---

45. Lauber, 39.

46. Lauber, 40.

47. The various reports of cannibalism are quite suspect, and there is scanty evidence to support cannibalism as a widespread occurrence. Nonetheless, slavers used the myth of cannibalism as a basis of comparison and an exoneration of European slavery.

48. Lauber, 40.

49. Lauber, 40–41

By ignoring the facility with which many Native American slaves integrated into enemy tribes, the colonial slave traders created and/or per-
petuated the impression that all Native American groups defined slavery
as a life-long condition. However, there were various ways in which slaves
gained liberty under the Native American system. Adoption was the primary mechanism, whereby a war captive joined the tribe. In some tribes,
"the adopted person became in every respect the peer of his fellow-tribes-
men. If he showed his ability he might become of high rank in the tribe"
while in other tribes such ascent was limited.[50] Slaves could also be ransomed.
Some tribes would swap enslaved captives for their own warriors, and
other tribes allowed the captives to work off a form of debt slavery that
more closely paralleled indenture.[51]

Equally important, the slave status was not inheritable in early Native
American systems of slavery. Whether their parents had been fully adopted
into the tribe or not, children of slaves had tribal membership: Seybert
notes that Creek children born to unions between slaves and tribal members became full members of the tribe. They fully incorporated into the group,
although E. A. S. Demers believes that their parents' origins may have
tainted their status. This distinction related more to prejudices against foreign lineage than to the slave status, although here the two are clearly in-
terwoven. The European model of slavery circumvented this path to liberty.
By claiming the precedent of the Native American system of slavery, yet ignoring its permeability, the European slavers mitigated the arguments
against their own slave practices.

Brooks says, "when the Spanish arrived, they were by no means shocked
at the indigenous captivity system. On the contrary, it was the one thing
about the New World that looked familiar."[52] Despite the discrepancies
noted above, there were several aspects of the Native American system that
resembled the Spanish, French, and English systems of bound service. Demers notes that "to French observers, captives who had neither been killed,
ransomed, nor adopted were equivalent in status to slaves, as their wills were
subject to a 'master.'"[53] In a travelogue entitled the "Journey of Dollier and
Galinee" (1669–1670), Demers finds evidence of early Native American
slavery as well as participation in the slave trade. When the writer Gali-

---

50. Lauber, 43.
51. Not all systems were this benign. Captives were often tortured and/or forced
to labor until they were sacrificed.
52. McLemee, 3.
53. Demers, 1.

nee requested that one of the Seneca Indians should act as a travel guide, the Seneca agreed to provide him with a slave-guide. Galinee also provided evidence of an early Native American slave trade by saying that the Seneca "begged us to wait until their people came back from the trade with the Dutch, to which they had taken all their slaves."[54]

The perception of the Native American slave system as equal to, or perhaps worse than, the European system persisted. This false representation allowed the colonial slave traders to claim they were in keeping with traditional tribal behavior. In other cases, colonial traders suggested that European slavery was an improvement from the native system. Although slaves in the Native American system could earn their freedom in a variety of ways, enter into tribal membership, and produce freeborn children, the misperceptions of Native American slavery spread. These misperceptions contributed to the lack of awareness of Native American enslavement. Since the European system was seen as a continuation, or even improvement, of the indigenous system, it drew little criticism. The colonial slave buyers were unaware of the distinctions between the systems, and it seemed that no public debates about this specific issue were conducted. Therefore, the lack of contemporaneous criticism has led to a modern scarcity of information about the enslavement of Native Americans throughout the European colonies.

A factor contributing to the shortage of material about the enslavement of Native Americans by the European settlers was its time period. Native American enslavement reached it height in the 1720s, slowed in the 1730s, and concluded, for the most part, by 1750. In Massachusetts, there were records listing Native American slaves well into the 18th Century,[55] but the numbers were few. Because their numbers had dwindled before the onset of the abolitionist movement, the enslaved Native Americans were omitted from the famous debates over slavery. It was only after Native American enslavement was on the wane that colonies began to feel the influence of the Enlightenment.

Native American slaves were not wholly without allies. Yet during the 1600s and 1700s such support was limited. The individuals and religious voices protesting against human exploitation were drowned out by the

---

54. Demers, 3.

55. Rick Green states that "for some Indians, servitude lasted only until age 24. But others were bound to masters for indefinite periods. Indian slaves and household servants appear on census rolls and court records well into the 18th century."

louder cry for cheap labor. One exception was that of William Penn, the Quaker from London, who approached his colonial settlement with a unique agenda. The desire for peace and parity with the native population of what is now New Jersey and Pennsylvania, the Lenni-Lenapé (the Delaware),[56] impelled a 1682 Treaty of Friendship.[57] Penn avoided conflict by purchasing native land at market rate[58] and ensuring that crimes committed between the groups would be judged by both native and settler representatives. Freedom of worship extended to all groups inclusive of the Unalachtico Lenape. Unfortunately, Penn's valuation of humanity, which extended to non-Christians, women, and Native Americans, excluded the natives of Africa: Penn traded and owned African slaves. Additionally other modern writers rejected the glorification of Penn as a member of an early anti-slavery coalition as well as the 2001 apologia for Quaker participation in reeducation programs and Indian Schools, such as Carlisle.[59]

Nonetheless, Penn and Quakers like him were instrumental in creating systems of fair exchange between the native and colonial people, and Pennsylvania sustained peaceful relations with the Delaware Indians far longer than other colonies were able to maintain with their neighboring tribes.[60] The strength of the relationship between the Delaware and the Quaker settlers survived Penn's returned to Europe in 1701. However, within two generations Pennsylvania became embroiled in a series of wars with the Iroquois, and Native American enslavement became a matter of course.

---

56. The Lenapé was comprised of three distinct groups: the Munsee, Unami, and Unalaqtgo. The Munsee were in the Upper Delaware, the Unami in the middle, and the Unalaqtgo occupied the land in the lower section. Penn's treaty was signed by various representatives, most notably the chief of the Unalaqtgo (Mooney, 1).

57. Although many sources, including Voltaire, refer to the treaty of 1682, only a 1701 treaty has the full extant text. Portions of treaties before 1701 also exist (Forrest, 1).

58. Market rate may have nonetheless been a reasonable price since the Iroquois had vacated much of the land that Penn purchased. "The French and their Native allies" had recently defeated the Iroquois, leaving the land which Penn desired vacant (Jennings, 205).

59. Amanda Keil, 3.

60. The intent of other colonial powers to enslave their neighbors was the leading cause for war between tribes and settlers as well as European orchestration of conflicts between tribes; therefore, Penn's eschewing of such tactics may contribute to his anti-slavery reputation.

In New England, the enslavement of Native Americans began as early as the 1630s. In Connecticut, it began almost with the founding of the colony and was in full swing by the end of the 1636 Pequot War. Margaret Newell states that by 1700, "New Englanders enslaved 2,000 Native Americans and sentenced hundreds more to long terms of servitude."[61] And Lauber notes that Native American slaves were "held in the colony before 1704. The records of Block Island show them there in sufficient numbers, in 1675, to warrant the town council regulating their action."[62] In 1680, a statement by the New York governor declared that "all Indians here have always been, and are, free, and not slave, *except* such as have been formerly brought from the Bay and Foreign Ports, [italics mine] ... This shows the presence of some Indian slaves in the Dutch colony."[63] Although there was ample evidence of the widespread use of Native Americans as slaves, as well as examples of Native American slaves in the 18th Century, the rapid increase in African slavery would soon curtail the use of Native Americans as slaves.

The reduction in Native American slavery prior to the onset of the abolitionist movement prevented its prevalence from receiving attention. Additionally, the fact that many tribes owned African slaves moved Native Americans from the position of the oppressed to that of the oppressor. Native Americans were left out of the intellectual and moral arguments against slavery; therefore, much of the documentation that focuses upon African slavery omits the Native American situation. There was a dearth of testimonies, newspaper, or pamphlet materials focused strictly upon the Native American condition in slavery. There were no slave narratives written by Native Americans that were on a par with the one written by Frederick Douglass.

Because the enslavement of Native Americans resulted in large part from conflict with Europeans or their native allies, the wars themselves were seen as a European concern over safety rather than a Native American quest for freedom. As stated above, the comparatively benign form of internal slavery practiced by many Native American groups devolved upon contact with Europeans. In order to provide the markets with slaves, various tribes waged war upon their neighbors with the express intent to gather prisoners of war to sell to the colonizers. However, the various large scale Indian Wars were contextualized in relation to the threats suffered by the Europeans. James Axtell suggested that "most scholars who refer to

---

61. Newell, 2.
62. Lauber,110.
63. Lauber, 112.

Indian history are primarily interested in the evolution of the dominant Anglo-American 'core culture' and political" situations.[64] Therefore, contemporaneous writers and scholars undervalued the impact of these wars upon the native populations as well as its influence upon the growing slave trade.

One prominent group involved in the Indian slave trade with the Europeans was the Westo[65] who at first lived in what is now northern Virginia and occupied lands in the Carolinas and Georgia. Upon their arrival in South Carolina, the Westo allied themselves with the British through a relationship with Dr. Henry Woodward, an agent of Lord Ashley one of the North Carolina's proprietors.[66] The Westo thrived while holding a lucrative three-year monopoly, which depended upon the sale of Indian slaves, "most of whom came from [Native American] nations allied with Spain."[67] Maintaining dominance throughout the region, they "became more successful in their slave raids in Georgia and Florida" and established a northern base to "facilitate trade with the English and French."[68] However, this distasteful success was short lived.

The Westo attempted to extend their trade monopoly for an additional 6 years, irritating the South Carolinians who wished to reduce their costs. As the Westo expanded their slave-catching net, competing tribes constrained them. Backed by the British,[69] these competing tribes then targeted the Westo. Ultimately, the Savannah and the Creek, an umbrella term encompassing several Native American groups, instigated the Westo War. Upon the Westo's defeat, many members of the Westo tribe went to Antigua as slaves, and the Savannahs replaced them as principal slavers in this region.[70]

The Carolinians had orchestrated the Westo War to break the Westo monopoly, rather than its ostensible cause of "a Westo attack on a small

---

64. Axtell, 982.

65. Documentation on the Westo is scanty. In his review of Eric E. Bowne's book, *Westo Indians: Slave Traders of the Early Colonial South*, Oliver Bielmann commends Bowne's work, stating: "Citing only nineteen direct references to the Westo Indians, Bowne does a fantastic job at recreating an unknown aspect of American history, the Indian slave trade during the seventeenth century" (158).

66. Avalon, 1.

67. Edgar, 86.

68. Bielmann, 158.

69. This is the period of the Beaver Wars, also called the French and Iroquois Wars, a 50-year span in which the Iroquois attempted to stretch their reach as far west as Ohio.

70. Seybert, 85.

costal nation."[71] Beyond breaking the Westo's control, this war increased the number of slaves because the Westo themselves became commodities. Shortly after this conflict, in 1664, North Carolina established regulations to monitor the Indian trade, which included goods as well as slaves. However, Governor Archdale moved to suppress the slave trade itself, with relative success. Yet, it was not until 1705 that the Commission for Indian Trade began its supervision and designated an agent to enforce its judgments.[72] One of its regulations made it illegal to enslave "free Indians,"[73] yet no previsions were made for the release of those already captured.

Farther south, the Creek moved on Spanish Florida. Tony Seybert estimates the Creeks' capture and sale of the Florida Indians to be 4,000 in a five-year period (1700–1705). In contrast, Gallay provided an estimate for the total number of Florida Indians sold during the 45-year period of 1670 to 1715 to be between 15,000 and 20,000. Seybert, however, noted that warfare and slavery eradicated many Florida groups; this pattern was then replicated in other regions, such as North Carolina where the Tuscarora, Yuchis, and Yamasee[74] were enslaved by the thousands.[75] Lauber, citing a 1708 report by Governor Nathaniel Johnson,[76] lists the enslaved native Americans: "Indian men slaves was given as 500, Indian women slaves, as 600, Indian children slaves, as 300, a total of 1400 Indian slaves. The number of negroes at the same time was stated as 4100, of indentured servants, 120, and of free whites, 3960."[77]

---

71. Seybert, 86.

72. The first Indian agent of South Carolina was named Thomas Nairne: "He prosecuted the governor's son-in law for enslaving friendly Cherokee" (Edgar, 99). The governor's response was to imprison Nairne on account of treason. Edgar notes Nairne's unfortunate demise years later during the Yamassee war.

73. Edgar, 99.

74. From 1711 to 1713, the Yamasee had allied with the British by capturing and enslaving the Tuscarora and Yuchis. However, the Yamasee's primacy soon ended as they too became enslaved and sold to islands.

75. Historian Alan Gallay estimates the number of Native Americans in southeast America sold in the British slave trade from 1670–1715 as between 24,000 and 51,000. He also notes that during this period more slaves (Native American, African, or otherwise) were exported from Charles Town than were imported.

76. Lauber cites Bancroft Papers Relating to Carolina, in New York City Public Library, MSS. vol. i, 1662–1769; Rivers, A Sketch of the History of South Carolina to the Close of the Proprietary Government, etc., p. 232; South Carolina Historical Society Collections, ii, p. 217; Thomas, The Indians of North America, etc., p. 95; Schaper, Sectionalism in South Carolina, p. 263.

77. Lauber, 106.

Farther west, as the British and French battled one another, the Chick-asaw—who, for the most part, were supported by the British—established extensive slaving practices. Their victims, the Choctaw, Arkansas, Tunicas, and Tawnsas, were allied with the French. The Chickasaw were predatory: "a single Chickasaw raid in 1706 on the Choctaw yielded 300 Indian captives for the English."[78] In response, the French armed the Natchez to war against the Chickasaw. Tragically, decades later the French were responsible for decimating rebellious Natchez in 1729. Gallay states that "the trade in Indian slaves was the most important factor effecting [sic] the South in the period 1679 to 1715: its impact was felt from Arkansas to the Carolinas and south to the Florida Keys." It is assuredly true that the Native American slave trade was the impetus for the Yamessee War.

Again, struggles over Native American trade and anger over widespread enslavement fuelled the conflict in which "all of the nations in the south east, with the exception of the Chickasaw and Cherokee, were united behind the leadership of the Lower Creek."[79] Violence swept through the region, and William Ramsey noted that "by 1718, when peace returned to much of the region, over four hundred colonists and an untold number of Native American warriors had perished, making the conflict a serious candidate for America's bloodiest war in proportion to the populations involved."[80] Edgar stated that "at no other time in Colonial American history, not even during King Philip's or the Pequot wars, did a colony face the danger that South Carolina did. The colonists were well aware of the threat to their existence but also to the empire."[81] Although the risk for the developing colony was reduced by the end of the Yamessee war, the fact remained that one of the causal factors, Indian enslavement, continued.

William Ramsey, in discussing the origins of the Yamessee War, provided the following analysis: "Incidents related to the Indian slave trade represented one of the most common categories of misconduct attributed to English traders. Six of the 30 complaints brought by Native Americans before the Commissioners of the Indian Trade in the five years preceding

---

78. Seybert, 89.
79. Edgar, 100.
80. Ramsey, 1.
81. Edgar notes that by the end of the conflicts in 1718, about 6 percent (400) of the colonist had been killed, the property loss estimate was £236,000 sterling, and defense had reached £116,000 sterling—"a sum more than three times the annual net value of exports over imports" (101).

the Yamasee War had to do with slavery."[82] He also notes that the "profitability of the slave trade, for native warriors as well as for English traders, placed individual liberties at risk across the South and led many to seek their victims among vulnerable friends and allies as well as legitimate enemies" (par. 25). A 1706 example of this occurred when a British trading group "attempted to augment its profits by having a small, English-allied, Indian nation called the Illcombees declared and taken as slaves en masse" (par. 35). Discussions of early colonial wars with Native Americans often overlook the contributory significance of events connected to the Native American slave trade and have led to its underrepresentation in much of the discussions of US slave history.

In keeping with the developments in Pennsylvania, the earlier settlements throughout New England, with varying degrees of success, followed a similar pattern in which the initial amity between the colonists and Native Americans devolved into violence and warfare. The most striking instance is that of the Algonquians in southern New England discussed above.

Throughout the period stemming from the Pequot War to King Phillip's War, the enslavement of women and children was de rigueur. Katz, in discussing a series of large conflicts between the colonial soldiers and the native Americans, explains that out of 200 people captured, the 22 or 24 adult males were executed, and "the remaining women and children, almost 80 percent of the total captured, were parceled up about evenly, as was common Indian practice, among the victorious Indian allies and the colonists of Massachusetts Bay."[83] Despite its lack of literary representation, the enslavement of Native Americans by the colonists and their tribal allies was practiced on a wide scale throughout the colonies. What captured the attention of writers were the other forms of legislated brutality carried out against the native people of America.

Moving from the colonial period into the 1800s, broken treaties and Indian removal were the issues which became represented in literature. One of the most significant events was that of the 1838–9 forced march of the Native American tribes across the mountains and the Mississippi River into Oklahoma. A recent representation of these events was presented in Robert J. Conley's fiction, *Mountain Windsong: A Novel of the Trail of Tears* which focused specifically upon the events faced by the Cherokee.

---

82. Ramsey, par. 25.
83. Katz, 219.

Although there were problems in the novel's construction, what is analyzed here are the ways this novel succeeds. In particular the novel wove together three different views and representations of the events surrounding Indian Removal and all were told from the perspective of Native Americans subjected to Jacksonian policy. The suffering of the people on the Trail of Tears, or the Trail Where They Cried which is a more accurate Cherokee translation, made up most of the novel's story.

The novel opened with an exchange between a grandfather and grandson. Grandpa called his grandson Cooj, the Cherokee word for boy, even though his name was Leroy and his nickname was Sonny. This term of endearment often signaled the opening of a storytelling session in which the tale of Oconeechee and Waguli was shared. The love affair between this young couple was disrupted by the 1835 Treaty of New Echota and its resultant relocation of the Cherokee across the Mississippi. Conley commented upon the laws and history of the period and connected them to a story evoking the traditional life destroyed by the US actions. He also linked this history to a modern rendition of a song set during the 1800s, called *Whippoorwill*, by combining the two main characters' names in his fiction with these poetic figures. Oconeechee's name was unchanged from the song, but Whippoorwill's name became Waguli in the novel.

Embedded in the text was the tribal conflict between the desire of some Cherokee to assimilate nontraditional ways and the commitment of others to tribal customs. This conflict was evident in the variety of ways the Cherokee of Georgia were conducting their lives prior to the removal. Many Cherokee had become fully entrenched in the western way of life in Georgia, owning productive business, adopting western garb, and intermarrying with European settlers. Others retained their traditional routines and lived seemingly harmoniously in the state. Within this section, the historical figures of John Ross, Elias Boudinot, and Major John Ridge were presented. The political conflict between Ross and the others was outlined, although the motivations of Boudinot and Ridge were described in myopically negative terms. In particular Ridge was presented as an economic mercenary willing to betray his people for the profitable exchange of land new territories.

Ridge did sign the Treaty of New Echota against the will of John Ross, the Cherokee tribal chief. Additionally he broke the Cherokee law that stated any tribal member who sold land outside of the tribe would be punished with death. Signing the agreement to cede their Georgia land to the US, Boudinot and Ridge went against the will of the people; however, their motivation may not have been the self-serving actions presented by Conley. Ridge was well aware of the possible repercussions of his actions. He left for the Oklahoma territory prior to the forced removal of 1838 and was to have said that his signing of the Treaty of New Echota was like signing his own death warrant.

Left out of Conley's narrative was that Ridge had been a ferocious warrior in his youth. Additionally, his candidacy as chief the Cherokee seemed assured until he himself stepped aside in support of Ross. Ridge, a full-blooded Cherokee, believe that Ross was better able to represent the nation because Ross was fluent in both Cherokee and English, being a child of parents from both nations. Instead Conley emphasized the fact that Ridge was among the wealthiest of the Cherokee, presenting it as a damning fact rather than a multifaceted condition. With removal, Ridge lost his farmland, totaling thousands of acres, which was some of the most profitable in Georgia. Relocation was not something he desired, but he recognized it as inevitable.

Nonetheless, his decision to avoid conflict and bloodshed by signing the treaty led to one of the most notable instances of cruelty suffered by Native American people: The forced march of the entire Cherokee tribe as well as other Native American groups crossed over 2,000 miles. It started badly and ended worse. Over 4000 individuals died during the trek to Oklahoma. Part of the problem was timing, part of the problem was the unexpectedly harsh weather, and part of the problem was the cruelty of some of the troops pushing the people forward. It was this last situation which Conley evokes most poignantly. The brutality of the soldiers, the treatment of women and children, and incarceration of warriors was described in horrific detail. Combined with these active attacks on the people were the passive assaults brought on by disease. Through his presentation, Conley commented directly upon President Andrew Jackson and his policies.

One character in *Windsong* is named Junaluska, which means "Tried But Failed." This character is based upon a historical figure who did in fact meet with the President to ask Jackson to discontinue his aggression. Junaluska believed that his prior relationship with Jackson would have held sway. Junaluska had been among the Cherokee allies to help Jackson's battalion defeat the Creek: interestingly, so had Major Ridge. Junaluska, more importantly, had saved Jackson's life during the battle of Horseshoe Bend, and Jackson had promised his undying friendship and protection. This was why Jackson's insistence upon removal was perceived as egregious betrayal of the Cherokee. The other aspect was that Jackson had overridden the 1832 Supreme Court decision which said that only the Federal government, and not the state of Georgia, could dictate terms of interaction with the Cherokee nation.

Jackson's pursuit of removal was in direct violation of the Supreme Court decision. Infamously, Jackson has been quoted or misquoted as saying, "Marshall has had his vote, now let him try to enforce it." Whether these words were ever uttered by Jackson is debatable, but his actions were clear. The forced removal of the Cherokee is the most recognized violence enacted against the Native American people, and Conley's work, as imperfect as it may be, ensured that the social, legal, inhuman atrocities remain part of the American literary conversations.

A direct inverse of ignorance about Native American enslavement, *The Trail of Tears* holds particular resonance in American consciousness. The notability of this one event, and its continued connection to the Cherokee people rather than the variety of tribes involved, was due to methods of communication. The Cherokee had been fully integrated members of the Georgian society prior to their expulsion. The Cherokee had developed their own syllabary in order to translate the Cherokee language into print. They produced their own documents including a newspaper, *The Cherokee Phoenix*, which Elias Boudinot edited. The people of the Cherokee nation had developed strong ties with the European community and there was a high degree of intermarriage. Some of the most prominent Cherokee families were related to the settler population in Georgia. Individuals such as John Ross, whose father was Scottish, self-selected to remain with the Cherokee while others moved deeper into Georgian culture. These people opted to stay as citizens of Georgia after the treaty of New Echota was signed whereas Ross followed his people across the Mississippi and into the new territory.

Because of this highly developed social structure, the Cherokee had the opportunity to leave a literary and historical legacy. They produced documents and pursued lawsuits that became a record of their experiences which could be shared and remembered. Other tribes were not as fortunate. Their stories were lost without the intervention of anthropologists such John Neihardt, who helped create *Black Elk Speaks*, an autobiographical account of an Oglala Sioux as translated from Lakota to English by Ben Black Elk. It is unclear what other tribal experiences have been lost, but it is clear that tribal reactions to broken treaties and settler actions vanished because of lack of documentation.

Other modern writers used the situation faced by various Native American groups throughout the 18th and 19th century as a backdrop to their cultural analysis. N. Scott Momaday's slim volume *The Way Rainy Moun-*

tain focused on a variety of events contributing to the decline of the Kiowa people and the despoiling of their culture. Interestingly his work had a tripartite structure that was used by Conley. Where Conley used the song of Whippoorwill, the fictional love story between Oconeechee and Wag-uli, in the legal documents of the *Worcester v. George* case and the Treaty of New Echota, Momaday presented one story in three voices. One version was a traditional tale of the events as told by Momaday's father, the second presented a more factual account, and the third version was in Momaday's own voice. In this section, Momaday shared his connections to past events and traced the impact of earlier history on contemporary lives. His descriptions often stemmed from personal memories and early stories, such as the mythical creation of the caldera of the Black Hills and the placement of the seven stars of Big Dipper. Embedded in the stories was the tale of one female slave who rose to prominence in the tribe. Although she comes from Mexico, rather than a more locally situated Native American population, her tale exemplified the liquidity of the slave status within the culture.

Within these incandescent stories were found comments and criticisms about the destruction of tradition. Other writers made similar connections and focused upon the corruption of the traditional world through the reservation system and the boarding school programs. Momaday commented upon the influence of western religion and the loss of traditional spirituality. In particular, the open spirituality of his grandmother was placed in counterpoint to the spiritually oppressed younger generation. These ideas tapped into the process of forced assimilation and religious conversion which took place on a grand scale through the educational process.

The intent of programs such as the Carlisle Indian Industrial School, which operated from 1879 to 1918, was to bring Native American children out of the territories for the purpose of educating them in western ways. The stated goal was to help the children in their transition from savage to civilized. What it actually did, according to the literary and historic voices, was rupture family connections without providing a coherent connection to the modern world. Many of the children of the boarding schools, although certainly not all, became lost between the two worlds available to them.

This feeling of disruption, dislocation, and disillusionment was not limited to the fictional or autobiographical accounts discussed above. Voices such as Black Elk addressed the time of change he experienced as a child. His stories told of the encroachment of the American frontiersmen and followed the movements of the military. A visionary and a profit,

Black Elk nonetheless remained firmly rooted in the real world events of his experiences. Philosophically interesting, Black Elk told stories in which the character of a man was developed less by his actions and more by his willingness to attempt them. This case was exemplified in the story he told of High Horse, a young man desperate to win a beautiful woman from her overly cautious father. After several attempts to impress him, all of which failed utterly, High Horse made a bold move of capturing horses from a neighboring tribe to deliver as either dowry or bribery. What came across in the story was not that High Horse had impressed the father with the number of horses, but instead, that High Horse had impressed the father because of his willingness to attempt something masculine, something risky, something worthwhile. This type of demonstration of personal worth was compromised by nontraditional value systems described by Black Elk.

The cultural conflicts discussed by Black Elk became more pervasive and problematic in the work of modern writers. In Sherman Alexie's collection of short stories, *Ten Little Indians*, the anxiety of dual citizenship, dual race, permeated the fiction. In one particularly conflicted moment seen in "Lawyer's League." Alexie presented Richard, a man with an African-American father and a Native American mother. Richard joked that he had received ancestry that would make him a generic superstar. He saw himself as a future leader of this tribe, of all Native Americans in fact. A member of the Spokane Indians in the Seattle area, Richard self-reported that he was both bright and ambitious; however, his internal conflicts and the legacy of racism plagued his life and destroy his career.

Richard planned to become a Senator and the first Native American representative of his tribe. In the early instances of the story, he told of a love relationship he allowed to evaporate because of his concern for his image. He worried that his political future would be undermined by a love affair or marriage to a white woman. He declined involvement with her believing that the racism of the American public would turn votes against him. This brief romantic encounter was connected to a basketball game. Here Richard confronted racism generated by his African American genetics which overrode his identification as Native American. The game ended badly and Richard came to blows with a white ball player. The narrative ended in a confused monologue to an imagined political constituency, in which he tried to explain his assault record. The close of the story sadly connected his inability to use his hand, broken in the brawl, to the loss of a nonexistent love affair, intertwining issues of race and the conflict of dual identification. Richard will remain forever caught between his iden-

tification as African-American and as Native American and he will ultimately fail to represent the Spokane people in the Senate. Themes of anxiety and disenfranchisement flow through Alexie's fiction. They trace back
to the legal and social structures robbing Native American people of their
traditional culture presented in earlier history and fiction.

In sum, the conflicts represented in the writings focused upon Native
American experience pay particular attention to the legal and social structures that disrupted traditional communities, took possession of Native
American lands, forced assimilation, and ultimately generated opposing
identities within the people who survived. Outside of the first Thanks-
giving, The Trail of Tears, and perhaps the Battle of Little Big Horn, much
of Native American history and the literature that represent it is relatively
unknown. Until modern writers focus upon issues such as Native American enslavement and the reeducation process, these events will remain
absent from general American consciousness.

Conclusion

Tracing through the literature representing the plight of European indentured servants, African slaves, and Native Americans, it becomes clear that legal customs and laws created structures that bound individuals to untenable conditions. Beginning with the earliest laws which codified the difference between the status of the servant and that of the slave, the mercenary qualities of colonial America and the early Republic can be seen in all its problematic glory.

As uncomfortable as these issues are, it must be remembered that the world of the 1600s and the 1700s was a cruel and inhospitable place. Infant and child mortality was high in both Europe and its American colonies during the 1700s, which pushed the life expectancy rate down to 35, or lower. Exceedingly hard work, poor nutrition, unsophisticated or unavailable health care, and disease were some of the influencing factors affecting the average American. Women, indentured servants, and slaves had an even shorter life span. The hardships faced by bound servants exemplified not only the cruelty of the age but also a different valuation of human life. The constant state of war, formally declared or otherwise, as well as the variety of diseases that plagued communities with their reoccurrence and ferocity, contributed to the precarious nature of human life. All this is not to say that an individual's partners, children, or friends were dismissible or unimportant. But when contrasted to modern times, the brutality of the age is noteworthy at both personal and institutional levels. Most significantly, the interaction between individuals in the hierarchical structures of earlier times was shockingly pitiless.

Perhaps most important is the difference between modern conceptions of individual human rights and the earlier concepts which allowed for the status of one's very humanity to be questioned. Descriptions which moved individuals into blurry categories of human or property, of servant or slave or savage, enabled divergent forms of treatment to develop. This is most clearly seen in the developing divide between the legal status of European indentured servants and African slaves. It is replicated in the ill-treatment offered the Native American population in general and the Native American slaves in particular. The contrast between the valued individual and the disposable one is further demonstrated by the physical cruelty to which these individuals were legally subjugated.

Long gone, thankfully, is the ability for individuals on the upper levels of social and industrial structures to legislate and to mete out physical punishments for subordinates. The plight of many of the early laborers in America and the hardships they faced have faded from public consciousness. Relegated to the annals of history or the files of defunct law, the suffering of indentured servants and Native American slaves and servants have only recently begun to be represented alongside the horrors faced by African slaves. Therefore, the potential for these experiences being lost is decreasing.

Modern writers are paying progressively more attention to the stories of individuals victimized through early colonial labor practices as well as the systems that abused laborers during the Republic's expansion. Increasingly stories of indentured servants are being shared in literature written about the early American labor system. These works are not intended to directly compare or compete with the experiences of African slaves but are intended to add to and enhance the understanding of the era of bound labor in America. These works, specifically through their use of law and their criticism of the larger social structures which allowed for systematic abuse, do much to highlight the underlying inequities embedded in the structures of power. The development of characters who function as indentured servants does much to draw attention to the abuse of such power and adds to the analysis of political and/or nationalistic agendas.

Using the Cromwellian "cleansing" of Ireland as well as earlier episodes in which the prisons of England were purged of their inmates, writers demonstrate how the indentured system was opportunistically abused for a twofold purpose. The first objective was to eradicate the unwanted people from Britain, and the second was to provide a labor supply for the expanding colonial presence in the New World. In these fictional works, as well as the letters and first-person narratives of the period, it is clear that the power of law was wielded only by the upper classes and the wealthy. Embodied in this fiction are the potentials for exploitation of the vulnerable underclass through the law as well as dramatic abuses of law itself. Heartrending letters written by indentured servants to their parents back home flesh out the realities of fictional narratives. The most poignant of these letters tell of the unexpected hardship and cruelty servants suffer at the hands of their masters. The lack of food, proper clothing, and inappropriate living accommodations was compounded by brutal working conditions and external threats of disease and warfare.

The fictional accounts which draw upon these legal and historic realities presented in the period's narratives emphasize the human suffering of servants. The situation faced by female indentured servants represents further injustices created by sexual abuse and reproductive coercion. Their vulnerability was heightened through their inability to self-represent in a court of law. One thing, however, unexplored in fiction and unmentioned in the narratives is sexual exploitation of men. Instances of such abuse certainly did happen but the resounding silence about the issue may be reflective of the age and the social taboos preventing descriptions about homosexual rape or female sexual abuse of men. The hierarchical structure of the servant system often placed a master, rather than a mistress, at the pinnacle with a secondary subsidiary male representative wielding power. In dramatic inversion, the lowest possible position in the structure was occupied by that of a woman, who not only had to contend with the authority of her master, or mistress, and/or overseer, but also had to negotiate the power exerted by the male members of her own class.

Embedded in male and female indentured servants' complaints about their status and the abuses they suffered was a condemnation of the mentality behind both public policy and individuals who used law to excuse the misuse of servants and slaves. Performance of cruelty in the guise of social correction or as a labor incentive was not limited, of course, to people in positions of power. However, these works developed the concept that the laws and the social structure of the period allowed sadistic natures to operate freely and they suggested that law and society encouraged these developments.

The works focusing on the brutality suffered by indentured servants often placed these characters on a continuum with the African slaves who suffered similar hardship. In some of these works, depending upon the period they reflected, a comparison was made: sometimes it was argued that indentured servants were treated more cruelly because their contracts had time limits and sometimes it was argued that the plight of the slaves was more horrific because of racial categorization as well as the legal differentiation of the chattel slavery. The historiography analyzing the treatment of slaves in contrast to servants tended to divide itself into similarly divergent streams when taking a position of comparison.

Projects invested in ranking atrocities are problematic for a host of reasons, not the least of which is the motivation to create such classifications. Nonetheless, both academic and narrative writings place a certain amount of attention on differentiating and comparing the situations faced by indentured servants and slaves. Native Americans are almost entirely omitted from these discussions. With that said, when looking at narrative reflections upon the experiences of these two groups, the views presented correspond to those argued by many academics.

One argument suggests that because an indentured servant's contract was time-limited, masters performed several bad acts to maximize their profit at the expense of the servant's welfare. The first provision in the legal contract was the requirement that servants be provided with proper nutrition to support them through their indenture. This seems to be one of the areas where costs were cut. Provisions, whether out of necessity or out of cruelty, seem to deteriorate as servants moved toward completion of their terms. One interpretation is that masters, knowing their servants were preparing to leave their employ, felt no compunction to provide for their workers' welfare. A more sinister reading suggests that masters were fully conscious of the servants' suffering and their own moneymaking activities became murderous. If servants did not complete their contract, the master was not obligated to pay the Freedom Dues mandated by law. The most obvious method of invalidating an indentured servant's contract was the death of the servant.

This analysis holds serious weight, but competing analysis suggests that even in this compromised situation, an indentured servant's treatment would have been on a par with the minimum levels of standard working practices of the age. This is not to suggest that working practices of the time were automatically positive or benevolent. There were many instances in which apprentices and other similarly vulnerable dependent laborers were cruelly treated by their employers. However, the indentured servants' position in the social structure may have eased their burdens, especially toward the culminating years of their contracts. Their impending freedom may have ensured that their treatment while in service remained tolerable. The servants, upon release, became fully integrated members of the community, and their previous status would have held no real social stigma. Depending on the time and location, as high as 85[1] percent of the citizenry was in bound service. This high percentage of individuals with past personal experience of life in service suggests that a certain amount of compassion would be extended to their successors. However, there was a grim reality that people who had suffered from a negative experience begrudged their successors if it seemed they had an easier time in the same situation. In instances such as these, the abuse suffered by onetime indentured servants may have caused them to treat their own servants cruelly.

What comes across in much of the literature fictionalizing this labor history is that indentured servants were closely linked to the status of slaves and they often suffered because of this parallel even though their contracts were time-limited and their status was elevated above the slaves. One of the most significant abuses suffered by indentured servants came in the form of law. The manipulation of contract time was the most often cited complaint and it was the most often depicted problem in representative fiction. The ways in which time was added to servant contracts, some claimed, made indentured servants as vulnerable if not more so than the slaves. Accusing and punishing servants for trumped up charges was one way that they could be punished with contract extension. Another situation, the one often faced by female servants, was the penalty for pregnancy. Fornication was against the contracts of all indentured servants, and proven accusations were punishable through a variety of mechanisms. Evidence of fornication, however, in terms of the physical exhibition of pregnancy was severely handled.

Women's contracts would be extended to compensate for whatever time was lost due to pregnancy. This time included any reduction in a woman's productivity during her baby's gestation, but much more significantly would be the compensations need to cover time lost during confinement and delivery. Added to this would be an extension of time lost due to recovery and childcare. Although indentured servants who fathered children were also penalized with time extension, paternity was often hard to prove. In part, the difficulty came from the lack of evidence. Because a woman would desperately try to protect her partner's identity in order to prevent the extension of the man's contract, women often hid their partner's name. Therefore, the burden of an indentured servant's pregnancy was most often only carried by the female servant. Gross exaggerations and overestimations of the time lost during a woman's confinement and other issues related to childbirth would increase a woman's indentured contracts anywhere from 2 to 4 years. This abuse of contract, as well as the female laborers themselves, parallels the situation of female slaves; however, the rewards masters received for their licentious deeds was significantly more enticing for the slave owner than it was for the indentured servant master.

Additionally, and ultimately more importantly, some masters would take advantage of the double profitability connected to an indentured servant's childbirth. Echoing Frederick Douglass' wording, whereby the master would not only enjoy the pleasure of the flesh but would also enjoy financially profit, the master would increase the woman's contract time by impregnating her. This is, however, where the parallel stops because a master of a slave would own his children born of slave women but not those of servants.

Masters who impregnated their slaves would later be able to sell these children, their children, for profit. This situation was included in almost every representation of slavery presented in fiction and included in many of the slave narratives generated at the time. The suffering of women and the children they brought into the world moved beyond analysis of the human condition and took issue with the law. Both the problematic development of law and its conflict with the Enlightenment thinkers, who had provided the basis for much of the intellectual framework that influenced conceptions of many of the Founders, is suggested in fictional representations of slavery. These imaginations take great pain to ensure that they are grounded in historical events and to make connections to legal realities. In fact, several of the more famous fictional accounts quote legal statutes and reflect and recount actual court cases in their representations.

Novels, first-person accounts, and other forms of narrative that address the conditions of African slaves help modern people to obtain a closer connection to the events in this early period. Additionally, many writers who reflect upon the experiences of the slaves pull their analysis forward to comment upon the social dynamics that created and supported the system and develop connections to the problems that stemmed from this initial injustice. Some of these narratives flow back and forth between the conditions of slavery and the situations faced by recently freed people. Others incorporate the conditions of other oppressed people into their narrative development. Increasingly, the presentation of indentured servants is found in novels set during the time of slavery. The incorporation of Native American characters is also on the rise, indicating that a vague awareness of this pairing has permeated the larger cultural context. However, most works of fiction focus upon one group of bound labor in isolation and comment upon the American legal system as it directly affects that specific situation.

This scenario is most clearly seen with fictional accounts focused upon Native Americans. These works tend to subdivide either into investigations of early colonial exploitation or into presentations of American expansion and the forced relocation and/or destruction of Native American culture and communities. Native American novels, short stories, and first-person narratives presented here focus upon the laws and treaties of these two periods. Significantly, when placed in a continuum, these works demonstrate a replication of broken treaties that stems as far back as the contact between the colonists and Eastern tribes. These early works emphasize the brutality of the age. And, they demonstrate the unreliable nature of the promises of amity offered by the colonists. The enslavement of native populations, the treacherous nature of alliances, and the ever changing nature of treaties and agreements echo throughout these works.

The question of savagery, or the description of Native Americans as savage, parallels the justification used by Europeans to exploit populations across the globe. The application of Christianity as a marker of civilization was a trope used to justify enslavement of Africans as well as Native Americans. Reeducation, or forced assimilation, was a byproduct of the earlier policies of cultural domination that spread to Native American peoples. The condition of individuals embroiled in bound labor, as well as the parallel policies that enable the systems to expand, seen in both law and fiction, demonstrates the unifying conditions of European indentured servants, African slaves, and Native American people.

Works Cited

Adams, Glenn. *Commemorating Brown: The Social Psychology of Racism and Discrimination*. 1st ed. Washington, DC: American Psychological Association, 2008.

Adjaye, Joseph K. "Amistad and the Lessons of History." *Journal of Black Studies* 29.3 (1999): 455–9.

Alexie, Sherman. *The Toughest Indian in the World*. New York: Grove Press, 2000.

Alpert, Jonathan L. "The Origin of Slavery in the United States—the Maryland Precedent." *The American Journal of Legal History* 14.3 (1970): 189–221.

Axtell, James. "Colonial America without the Indians: Counterfactual Reflections." *The Journal of American History* 73.4 (1987): 981–96.

Baron, Jane B. "Law, Literature, and the Problems of Interdisciplinarity." *The Yale Law Journal* 108.5 (1999): 1059–85.

Beckles, Hilary McD. "Historicizing Slavery in West Indian Feminisms." *Feminist Review*.59, Rethinking Caribbean Difference (1998): 34–56.

Beckles, Hilary. *White Servitude and Black Slavery in Barbados, 1627–1715*. 1st ed. Knoxville: University of Tennessee Press, 1989.

Bell, Bernard W. "Beloved: A Womanist Neo-Slave Narrative; Or Multivocal Remembrances of Things Past." *African American Review* 26.1, Women Writers Issue (1992): 7–15.

Berlak, Ann. "Teaching and Testimony: Witnessing and Bearing Witness to Racisms in Culturally Diverse Classrooms." *Curriculum Inquiry* 29.1 (1999): 99–127.

Birmingham, David. "Review: Joseph Miller's Way of Death." *Past and Present*.131 (1991): 204–16.

"Breaking the Chains; Slavery." *The Economist* February 24 2007.

Brophy, Alfred L. "'Over and Above … there Broods a Portentous Shadow,—the Shadow of Law': Harriet Beecher Stowe's Critique of Slave Law in 'Uncle Tom's Cabin.'" *Journal of Law and Religion* 12.2 (1995): 457–506.

Brown, Cecil, and Toni Morrison. *Interview with Toni Morrison*. Vol. 36., 1995.

Brown, Kathleen M., and Institute of Early American History and Culture. *Good Wives, Nasty Wenches, and Anxious Patriarchs: Gender, Race, and Power in Colonial Virginia*. Chapel Hill: Published for Institute of Early American History and Culture by University of North Carolina Press, 1996.

Calarco, N. Joseph. "Production as Criticism: Miller's 'the Crucible.'" *Educational Theatre Journal* 29.3 (1977): 354–61.

Carroll, Rebecca, and Booker T. Washington. *Uncle Tom Or New Negro?: African Americans Reflect on Booker T. Washington and Up from Slavery One Hundred Years Later*. 1st ed. ed. New York: Broadway Books/Harlem Moon, 2006.

Catterall, Helen Tunnicliff, and James J. Hayden. *Judicial Cases Concerning American Slavery and the Negro*. New York: Octagon Books, 1968.

Cave, Alfred A. "Who Killed John Stone? A Note on the Origins of the Pequot War." *The William and Mary Quarterly* 49.3 (1992): 509–21.

Cavanaugh, James F. *Irish Slavery*. http://www.raceandhistory.com/cgi-bin/forum/webbbs_config.pl/noframes/read/1638.

Center of Military History. *Black Soldier, White Army*. Washington, DC: Center of Military History, 1997.

Coonradt, Nicole M. "To be Loved: Amy Denver and Human Need: Bridges to Understanding in Toni Morrison's 'Beloved.'" *College Literature* 32.4 (2005): 168–87.

Cozzens, Lisa. "The Civil Rights Movement 1955–1965." African American History. http://fledge.watson.org/~lisa/blackhistory/civilrights-55–65 (25 May 1998).

Cromwell, Oliver. "A Proclamation by His Highness and the Parliament." London: Printed by Henry Hills and John Field, 1657.

Culbertson, Roberta. "Embodied Memory, Transcendence, and Telling: Recounting Trauma, Re-Establishing the Self." *New Literary History* 26.1, Narratives of Literature, the Arts, and Memory (1995): 169–95.

Cunnigen, Donald, Rutledge M. Dennis, and Myrtle Gonza ZZ Glascoe, eds. *The Racial Politics of Booker T. Washington Myrtle Gonza Glascoe*. Amsterdam; Boston, Mass.: Elsevier JAI, 2006.

Dargis, Manohla. "The Imperfect Soul Who Helped Bring an End to the Slave Trade." *The New York Times* February 23 2007, sec. E; PT1; Movies, Performing Arts/Weekend Desk; Film Review: 10.

Davis, T. R. "Negro Servitude in the United States: Servitude Distinguished from Slavery." *The Journal of Negro History* 8.3 (1923): 247–83.

Dayal, Samir. "Postcolonialism's Possibilities: Subcontinental Diasporic Intervention." *Cultural Critique*. 33 (1996): 113–49.

Degler, Carl N. "Slavery and the Genesis of American Race Prejudice." *Comparative Studies in Society and History* 2.1 (1959): 49–66.

_____. "Slavery in Brazil and the United States: An Essay in Comparative History." *The American Historical Review* 75.4 (1970): 1004–28.

DeLombard, Jeannine Marie. *Slavery on Trial: Law, Abolitionism, and Print Culture.* Chapel Hill: University of North Carolina Press, 2007.

Deloria, Philip Joseph, and Neal Salisbury. *A Companion to American Indian History.* Vol. [4]. Malden, MA: Blackwell Publishing, 2004.

Deloria, Vine. *Custer Died for Your Sins: An Indian Manifesto.* Norman: University of Oklahoma Press, 1988.

Demers, E. A. S. "Native-American Slavery and Territoriality in the Colonial Upper Great Lakes Region." *Michigan Historical Review* 28.2 (2002): pp. 163–172.

Denard, Carolyn, and Carolyn Denard. *Blacks, Modernism, and the American South: An Interview with Toni Morrison.* Vol. 31., 1998.

Diggins, John P. "Slavery, Race, and Equality: Jefferson and the Pathos of the Enlightenment." *American Quarterly* 28.2, Special Issue: An American Enlightenment (1976): 206–28.

Diggs, Ellen Irene. *Black Chronology from 4000 B.C. to the Abolition of the Slave Trade.* Boston, Mass.: G.K. Hall, 1983.

Douglass, Frederick, W. E. B. Du Bois, and Booker T. Washington. *Three African-American Classics.* Dover ed. Mineola, N.Y.: Dover Publications, 2007.

Douglass, Frederick, et al. *The Heritage Series.* Grand Rapids, Mich.: Candace Press, 1996.

_____. *Narrative of the Life of Frederick Douglass, an American Slave.* Cambridge, Mass.: Belknap Press, 1960.

Douglass, John E. "Power of Attorneys: Formation of Colonial South Carolina's Attorney System, 1700–1731." *The American Journal of Legal History* 37.1 (1993): 1–24.

Draper, Sharon M. *Copper Sun.* 1st ed. New York: Atheneum Books for Young Readers, 2006.

Dreifus, Claudia. *Chloe Wofford Talks about Toni Morrison.(Magazine Desk) (Interview),* 1994.

Drescher, Seymour. *Capitalism and Antislavery: British Popular Mobilization in Comparative Perspective.* New York: Oxford University Press, 1987.

_____. *The Mighty Experiment: Free Labor Vs. Slavery in British Emancipation.* New York: Oxford University Press, 2002.

Du Bois, W. E. B., et al. *African American Political Thought, 1890–1930: Washington, Du Bois, Garvey, and Randolph by Cary D. Wintz.* Armonk, NY: M.E. Sharpe, 1996.

Du Plessis, Max, and Steve Pete. *Repairing the Past?: International Perspectives on Reparations for Gross Human Rights Abuses.* Vol. 1. Antwerpen; Holmes Beach, Fla.: Intersentia; Distribution for North America, Gaunt, 2007.

Dubin, Steven C. "Symbolic Slavery: Black Representations in Popular Culture." *Social problems* 34.2 (1987): 122–40.

Dubos, Alain. *La Baie Des Maudits: Roman.* Paris: Presses de la cité, 2006.

Dubos, René J. *Beast Or Angel? Choices that make Us Human.* New York: Scribner, 1974.

Dussere, Erik. "Accounting for Slavery: Economic Narratives in Morrison and Faulkner." *MFS Modern Fiction Studies* 47.2 (2001): 329–55.

Eisenberg, Jose. "Antonio Vieira and the Justification of Indian Slavery." *Luso-Brazilian Review* 40.1, Special Issue: Antonio Vieira and the Luso-Brazilian Baroque (2003): 89–95.

Emancipation Proclamation, January 1, 1863. "Presidential Proclamations, 1791–1991." Record Group 11; General Records of the United States Government; National Archives.

Engerman, Stanley L. "The Slave Trade and British Capital Formation in the Eighteenth Century: A Comment on the Williams Thesis." *The Business History Review* 46.4 (1972): 430–43.

Eyerman, Ron. "The Past in the Present: Culture and the Transmission of Memory." *Acta Sociologica* 47.2 (2004): 159–69.

Ferguson, Sally Ann H. "Christian Violence and the Slave Narrative." *American Literature* 68.2 (1996): 297–320.

Finkelman, Paul. *The African Slave Trade and American Courts: The Pamphlet Literature.* Vol. ser. 5. New York: Garland Pub., 1988.

——. "Evading the Ordinance: The Persistence of Bondage in Indiana and Illinois." *Journal of the Early Republic* 9.1 (1989): 21–51.

——. "James Madison and the Bill of Rights: A Reluctant Paternity." *The Supreme Court Review* 1990 (1990): 301–47.

——. "The Kidnapping of John Davis and the Adoption of the Fugitive Slave Law of 1793." *The Journal of Southern History* 56.3 (1990): 397–422.

——. "On Cinque and the Historians." *The Journal of American History* 87.3 (2000): 940–6.

——. "Slavery and the Northwest Ordinance: A Study in Ambiguity." *Journal of the Early Republic* 6.4 (1986): 343–70.

_____. "Slaves as Fellow Servants: Ideology, Law, and Industrialization." *The American Journal of Legal History* 31.4 (1987): 269–305.

Fish, Stanley Eugene. *Doing what Comes Naturally: Change, Rhetoric, and the Practice of Theory in Literary and Legal Studies.* Durham, NC: Duke University Press, 1989.

Fitts, Dudley. *Greek Plays in Modern Translation.* New York: Dial Press, 1947.

Fogleman, Aaron S. "From Slaves, Convicts, and Servants to Free Passengers: The Transformation of Immigration in the Era of the American Revolution." *The Journal of American History* 85.1 (1998): 43–76.

Foreman, P. Gabrielle (Pier Gabrielle). " 'Reading Aright': White Slavery, Black Referents, and the Strategy of Histotextuality in Iola Leroy." *The Yale Journal of Criticism* 10.2 (1997): 327–54.

Foster, David William. "Spanish, American and Brazilian Literature: A History of Disconsonance." *Hispania* 75.4, The Quincentennial of the Columbian Era (1992): 966–78.

Fox, James Alan, and Jack Levin. "Multiple Homicide: Patterns of Serial and Mass Murder." *Crime and Justice* 23 (1998): 407–55.

Frank, Andrew. *The Birth of Black America: The Age of Discovery and the Slave Trade.* New York: Chelsea House, 1996.

Amistad. Dir. Freeman, Morgan, Nigel Hawthorne, and Anthony Hopkins. DreamWorks, 1999.

Fuller, Alexandra. *Don't Let's Go to the Dogs Tonight: An African Childhood.* 1st ed. New York: Random House, 2002.

Galenson, David W. "British Servants and the Colonial Indenture System in the Eighteenth Century." *The Journal of Southern History* 44.1 (1978): 41–66.

_____. "The Market Evaluation of Human Capital: The Case of Indentured Servitude." *The Journal of Political Economy* 89.3 (1981): 446–67.

_____. "The Rise and Fall of Indentured Servitude in the Americas: An Economic Analysis." *The Journal of Economic History* 44.1 (1984): 1–26.

_____. "White Servitude and the Growth of Black Slavery in Colonial America." *The Journal of Economic History* 41.1, The Tasks of Economic History (1981): 39–47.

Gardner, John. *Jason and Medeia.* New York: Knopf; distributed by Random House, 1973.

Gates, Gordon S. "Teaching-Related Stress: The Emotional Management of Faculty." *The Review of Higher Education* 23.4 (2000): 469–90.

Gelb, Barbara. *Varnished Brass: The Decade After Serpico.* New York: Putnam, 1983.

Geiser, Karl Frederick. *Redemptioners and Indentured Servants In The Colony of Common Wealth Of Pennsylvania*. The Tuttle, Morehouse & Taylor. New Haven, 1901.

Genovese, Eugene D. *Roll, Jordan, Roll; the World the Slaves made*. New York: Pantheon Books, 1974.

Gilbert, Olive, Sojourner Truth, and Nell Irvin Painter. *Narrative of Sojourner Truth: A Bondswoman of Olden Time, with a History of Her Labors and Correspondence Drawn from Her Book of Life; also, A Memorial Chapter*. New York, N.Y.: Penguin Books, 1998.

Gross, Ariela J. "Beyond Black and White: Cultural Approaches to Race and Slavery." *Columbia Law Review* 101.3 (2001): 640–90.

_____. *Double Character: Slavery and Mastery in the Antebellum Southern Courtroom*. Princeton, N.J.: Princeton University Press, 2000.

_____. "Litigating Whiteness: Trials of Racial Determination in the Nineteenth-Century South." *The Yale Law Journal* 108.1 (1998): 109–88.

_____. *What Blood Won't Tell: A History of Race on Trial in America*. Cambridge, Mass.: Harvard University Press, 2008.

Grubb, Farley. "The Market for Indentured Immigrants: Evidence on the Efficiency of Forward-Labor Contracting in Philadelphia, 1745–1773." *The Journal of Economic History* 45.4 (1985): 855–68.

_____. "The Transatlantic Market for British Convict Labor." *The Journal of Economic History* 60.1 (2000): 94–122.

Guerry, William A. "Harriet Beecher Stowe." *The Sewanee Review* 6.3 (1898): 335–44.

Guild, June (Purcell). *Black Laws of Virginia; a Summary of the Legislative Acts of Virginia Concerning Negroes from Earliest Times to the Present*. New York: Negro Universities Press, 1969.

Gunning, Sally. *Bound*. New York: Harper, 2008.

Haberly, David T. "Abolitionism in Brazil: Anti-Slavery and Anti-Slave." *Luso-Brazilian Review* 9.2 (1972): 30–46.

Harjo, Suzan Shown. "American Indian Religious Freedom Act After Twenty-Five Years: An Introduction." *Wicazo Sa Review* 19.2, Colonization/Decolonization, I (2004): 129–36.

Hall, Kermit L. ed. The Oxford Companion to American Law. Oxford UP, Oxford. 2002.

Harlan Jacobson. "Screen Deities Float about Annual Cannes Film Festival." *USA Today*.

Hay, Douglas, and Paul Craven. *Masters, Servants, and Magistrates in Britain and the Empire, 1562–1955*. Chapel Hill: University of North Carolina Press, 2004.

Heavner, Robert O. "Indentured Servitude: The Philadelphia Market, 1771–1773." *The Journal of Economic History* 38.3 (1978): 701–13.

Henning, Joseph M. *Outposts of Civilization: Race, Religion, and the Formative Years of American-Japanese Relations.* New York: New York University Press, 2000.

Herrick, Cheesman A. *White Servitude in Pennsylvania: Indentured and Redemption Labor in Colony and Commonwealth.* Philadelphia, Pennsylvania: John Joseph McVey, 1926.

Hoofard, Jennifer. *An Interview with Toni Morrison: "Thinking about a Story".* Vol. 17., 2007.

Hurston, Zora Neale. *Their Eyes were Watching God: A Novel.* Urbana: University of Illinois Press, 1978.

"Intergovernmental Compacts in Native American Law: Models for Expanded Usage." *Harvard law review* 112.4 (1999): 922.

Jacobs, Harriet A., Lydia Maria Francis Child, and Jean Fagan Yellin. *Incidents in the Life of a Slave Girl: Written by Herself.* Cambridge, Mass.: Harvard University Press, 1987.

Jacobs, J. U. "Nadine Gordimer's Intertextuality: Authority and Authorship in 'My Son's Story'." *English in Africa* 20.2 (1993): pp. 25–45.

James, Joy. *Imprisoned Intellectuals: America's Political Prisoners Write on Life, Liberation, and Rebellion.* Lanham, Rowman & Littlefield, 2003.

Jarvis, Michael J. "Maritime Masters and Seafaring Slaves in Bermuda, 1680–1783." *The William and Mary Quarterly* 59.3, Slaveries in the Atlantic World (2002): 585–622.

Johnston, J. H. "The Mohammedan Slave Trade." *The Journal of Negro History* 13.4 (1928): 478–91.

Huston, James L. "Reconstruction as It Should Have Been: An Exercise in Counterfactual History." *Civil War History.* 51:4 (2005): 358–363.

Katz, Steven T. "The Pequot War Reconsidered." *The New England Quarterly* 64.2 (1991): 206–24.

Kawash, Samira. "Haunted Houses, Sinking Ships: Race, Architecture, and Identity in Beloved and Middle Passage." *CR: The New Centennial Review* 1.3 (2003): 67–86.

Krell, David Farrell. "The Bodies of Black Folk: From Kant and Hegel to Du Bois and Baldwin." *Boundary* 2 27.3 (2000): 103–34.

Krumholz, Linda. "The Ghosts of Slavery: Historical Recovery in Toni Morrison's Beloved." *African American Review* 26.3, Fiction Issue (1992): 395–408.

Lee, Christopher J. "Review: [Untitled]." *The International Journal of African Historical Studies* 37.3 (2004): 568–70.

MacDonald, Christine. "Judging Jurisdictions: Geography and Race in Slave Law and Literature of the 1830s." *American Literature* 71.4 (1999): 625–55.

Martin, Wm H. "Hening and the Statutes at Large." *The Virginia Law Register* 13.1 (1927): 25–37.

McCafferty, Kate. *Testimony of an Irish Slave Girl.* New York: Viking, 2002.

McClendon, R. Earl. "The Amistad Claims: Inconsistencies of Policy." *Political Science Quarterly* 48.3 (1933): 386–412.

McDermott, Gerald R. "Jonathan Edwards and American Indians: The Devil Sucks their Blood." *The New England Quarterly* 72.4 (1999): 539–57.

McLaurin, Melton Alonza. "On Infanticide, the Peculiar Institution, and Public Memory." *Reviews in American History* 27.2 (1999): 250–3.

Miles, Tiya. *Uncle Tom was an Indian: Tracing the Red in Black Slavery.* Modern Language Association of America.

Minges, Patrick. "Beneath the Underdog: Race, Religion, and the Trail of Tears." *The American Indian Quarterly* 25.3 (2001): 453–79.

Molly Dragiewicz. "Teaching about Trafficking: Opportunities and Challenges for Critical Engagement." *Feminist Teacher* 18.3 (2008): 185–201.

Momaday, N. Scott, and Al Momaday. *The Way to Rainy Mountain.* 1st ed. Albuquerque: University of New Mexico Press, 1969.

Momaday, Natachee Scott. *House made of Dawn.* New York: Harper & Row, 1968.

Moraley, William, Billy Gordon Smith, and Susan E. Klepp. *The Infortunate: The Voyage and Adventures of William Moraley, an Indentured Servant.* University Park, Pa.: Pennsylvania State University Press, 1992.

Morrison, Toni, and Nellie McKay. *An Interview with Toni Morrison.* Vol. 24., 1983.

Morrison, Toni. *Beloved: A Novel.* Gift ed. New York: Knopf: Distributed by Random House, 1998.

———. *Playing in the Dark: Whiteness and the Literary Imagination.* Vol. 1990. Cambridge, Mass.: Harvard University Press, 1992.

———. *Song of Solomon.* New York: Knopf, 1977.

———. *Sula.* 1st ed. New York: Knopf; distributed by Random House, 1974.

———. *Tar Baby.* New York: Knopf: distributed by Random House, 1981.

Muss-Arnolt, W. "The Babylonian Account of Creation." *The Biblical World* 3.1 (1894): 17–27.

Nicholson, Bradley J. "Legal Borrowing and the Origins of Slave Law in the British Colonies." *The American Journal of Legal History* 38.1 (1994): 38–54.

Noble, Marianne. *The Masochistic Pleasures of Sentimental Literature.* Princeton, N.J.: Princeton University Press, 2000.

Okur, Nilgun Anadolu. "Underground Railroad in Philadelphia, 1830–1860." *Journal of Black Studies* 25.5 (1995): 537–57.

Olien, Michael D. "After the Indian Slave Trade: Cross-Cultural Trade in the Western Caribbean Rimland, 1816–1820." *Journal of Anthropological Research* 44.1 (1988): 41–66.

Ouologuem, Yambo. *Bound to Violence.* 1st ed. New York: Harcourt Brace Jovanovich, 1971.

Petar Ramadanovic. "'You Your Best Thing, Sethe': Trauma's Narcissism." *Studies in the Novel* 40. 1–2 (2008): 178–88.

Pollak, Louis. *Race, Law History the Supreme Court from "Dred Scott" to "Grutter v. Bollinger".* Vol. 134., 2005.

Posner, Richard A. *Economic Analysis of Law.* 2d ed. Boston: Little, Brown, 1977.

_____. *Law and Literature: A Misunderstood Relation.* Cambridge, Mass.: Harvard University Press, 1988.

_____. *The Problems of Jurisprudence.* Cambridge, Mass.: Harvard University Press, 1990.

Quarles, Benjamin. "Frederick Douglass and the Woman's Rights Movement." *The Journal of Negro History* 25.1 (1940): 35–44.

Rael, Patrick. "Why this Film about Slavery?" *The History Teacher* 31.3 (1998): 387.

Ramsey, William L. "'Something Cloudy in their Looks': The Origins of the Yamasee War Reconsidered." *The Journal of American History* 90.1 (2003): 44–75.

Ranlet, Philip. "Another Look at the Causes of King Philip's War." *The New England Quarterly* 61.1 (1988): 79–100.

Rediker, Marcus. "'Under the Banner of King Death': The Social World of Anglo-American Pirates, 1716 to 1726." *The William and Mary Quarterly* 38.2 (1981): 203–27.

Reimers, David M., and Frederick M. Binder. *The Way we Lived: Essays and Documents in American Social History.* Lexington, Mass.: D.C. Heath, 1988.

Riddell, William Renwick. "A Half-Told Story of Real White Slavery in the Seventeenth Century." *Journal of the American Institute of Criminal Law and Criminology* 21.2 (1930): 247–53.

Riss, Arthur. *Race, Slavery, and Liberalism in Nineteenth-Century American Literature.* New York: Cambridge U P, 2006.

Robbins, Sarah. "Gendering the History of the Antislavery Narrative: Jux-
taposing Uncle Tom's Cabin and Benito Cereno, Beloved and Middle
Passage." *American Quarterly* 49.3 (1997): 531–73.

Roe, Melissa. "Differential Tolerances and Accepted Punishments for Disobedient Indentured Servants and Their Masters in Colonial Court."
http://eh.net/Clio/Publications/indentured.shtml.

Sainsbury, John A. "Indian Labor in Early Rhode Island." *The New England
Quarterly* 48.3 (1975): 378–93.

Sainsbury, Noel W. (Editor). "America and West Indies: December 1661."
Calendar of State Papers Colonial, America and West Indies, Volume
5: 1661–1668 (1880): 61–66.

Scott, Rebecca J. "The Atlantic World and the Road to Plessy v. Ferguson,"
Journal of American History. 94 (2007): 726–733.

Sharon Holm. "The 'Lie' of the Land: Native Sovereignty, Indian Literary
Nationalism, and Early Indigenism in Leslie Marmon Silko's *Cere-
mony*." *The American Indian Quarterly* 32.3 (2008): 243–74.

Silko, Leslie. *Gardens in the Dunes: A Novel*. New York: Simon & Schus-
ter, 1999.

Sio, Arnold A. "Interpretations of Slavery: The Slave Status in the Americas." *Comparative Studies in Society and History* 7.3 (1965): 289–308.

Smith, Abbot Emerson. *Colonists in Bondage; White Servitude and Convict Labor in America, 1607–1776*. Gloucester, Mass.: P. Smith, 1965.

Smith, Warren B. *White Servitude in Colonial South Carolina*. Columbia:
University of South Carolina Press, 1961.

Souden, David. "'Rogues, Whores and Vagabonds'? Indentured Servant
Emigrants to North America, and the Case of Mid-Seventeenth-Cen-
tury Bristol." *Social History* 3.1 (1978): 23–41.

Steele, Ian Kenneth. "Exploding Colonial American History: Amerindian,
Atlantic, and Global Perspectives." *Reviews in American History* 26.1
(1998): 70–95.

Smith, W.B., *White Servitude in Colonial South Carolina*. U of South Carolina P, Columbia, 1961.

Storhoff, Gary. "'Anaconda Love': Parental Enmeshment in Toni Morrison's Song of Solomon." *Style*. 31.2 (1997). 290–309.

Stowe, Harriet Beecher. *Uncle Tom's Cabin, Or, Life among the Lowly*. New
York: Viking P, 1982.

Sylvester, Melvin. The African American: A Journey from Slavery to Freedom. http://www.cwpost.edu/cwis/cwp/library/aaslavry.htm.

"Surprise! the Earliest Place Blacks Attained Equality with Whites was on
a Pirate Ship." *The Journal of Blacks in Higher Education*.28 (2000): 56.

Tolnay, Stewart E., E. M. Beck, and James L. Massey. "Black Competition and White Vengeance: Legal Execution of Blacks as Social Control in the Cotton South, 1890 to 1929." *Social Science Quarterly.* 73(3): 627–644.

Velie, Alan R. *Four American Indian Literary Masters: N. Scott Momaday, James Welch, Leslie Marmon Silko, and Gerald Vizenor.* 1st ed. Norman: University of Oklahoma Press, 1982.

Viramontes, Helena María. *Under the Feet of Jesus.* New York: Dutton, 1995.

Virginia Company of London, Susan Myra Kingsbury, and Library of Congress. *The Records of the Virginia Company of London.* Washington: Govt. Print. Off., 1906.

Williams, E. http://www.ewtn.com/library/HUMANITY/SLAVES.TXT.

Weisenberger, Steven. "A Historical Margaret Garner." http://www.margaretgarner.org/essays.html.

Waskow, Arthur I. *From Race Riot to Sit-in, 1919 and the 1960s; a Study in the Connections between Conflict and Violence.* Gloucester, Mass.: Peter Smith, 1975.

Wiecek, William M. "Somerset: Lord Mansfield and the Legitimacy of Slavery in the Anglo-American World." *The University of Chicago Law Review* 42.1 (1974): 86–146.

Wilkinson, Charles F. *American Indians, Time, and the Law: Native Societies in a Modern Constitutional Democracy.* New Haven: Yale University Press, 1987.

Wilmer, Harry A. "Odyssey of a Psychotherapist." *Science* 145.3635 (1964): 902–3.

Wilson, Ruth Danenhower. "Justifications of Slavery, Past and Present." *The Phylon Quarterly* 18.4 (1957): 407–12.

Wintz, Cary D. *African American Political Thought, 1890–1930: Washington, Du Bois, Garvey, and Randolph.* Armonk, N.Y.: M.E. Sharpe, 1996.

Zaeske, Susan. *Signatures of Citizenship: Petitioning, Antislavery, and Women's Political Identity.* Chapel Hill: University of North Carolina Press, 2003.

Index